# FRANCE

## MEDITERRANEAN CUISINE

# FRANCE
## MEDITERRANEAN CUISINE

KÖNEMANN

# Contents

# List of Recipes

Difficulty:

★      Easy
★★    Medium
★★★   Difficult

## Hot Appetizers 28

## Cold Appetizers 8

## Soups 64

## Fish & Seafood  82

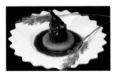

## Desserts & Pastries  154

## Meat & Poultry  122

# Cold Appetizers

# Langoustine Carpaccio

Preparation time: 40 minutes
Chilling time: 20 minutes
Cooking time: 20 minutes
Difficulty: ★

**Serves 4**

| | |
|---|---|
| 12 | fresh langoustines |
| 2 bundles | asparagus spears |
| 6 tbsp | olive oil |
| 4 | oranges |

| | |
|---|---|
| 1 | lemon |
| 1 bunch | fresh tarragon |
| 1 tsp | coarse grain mustard |
| | salt |
| | pepper |
| few sprigs | fresh dill |

This recipe is summer on a plate! We owe a big thank-you to Italian artist Vittore Carpaccio, who gave his name to this refreshing appetizer. This low-calorie appetizer is easy to prepare.

Alain Carro prefers langoustines because the flesh soaks up the flavors of the other ingredients wonderfully well, but these shellfish have been chosen for their attractive color too. The langoustines must be absolutely fresh, with shining, black eyes and a pleasant, unobtrusive smell. If langoustines are not available, our chef advises using mackerel fillets. They are equally suitable for this recipe and are much cheaper! If you ask your fishmonger to slice the fillets, you will get the very thin slices you want. Where freshness is concerned, the same applies to mackerel, with its rainbow scales, as to the langoustines. Remove all the little bones with tweezers.

Asparagus, which heralds the warmer time of year, is widely grown in the south of France. The spears should be straight. Bear in mind that asparagus keeps for up to three days only but, depending on the time of year, you can, of course, use white asparagus. Before peeling, rinse the spears in hot water. Generally, asparagus is cooked in boiling, salted water for 5–10 minutes, depending on the spears' thickness. After cooking, the asparagus can be placed in a bowl of ice water so that it cools down quickly.

The tarragon used to flavor the olive oil is chopped finely. You should always use this herb fresh; if you can't find fresh tarragon you could use fresh chervil. If you want to use the langoustine heads as a garnish for this appetizer you must blanch them first.

*Peel the langoustines and slice them open lengthwise. Spread them out and remove the black intestines. Meanwhile, bring a pan of salted water to the boil, add the asparagus, and simmer for 5–10 minutes. Drain the asparagus and leave it to cool.*

*Spread out a large piece of plastic wrap. Brush half the wrap with a little of the olive oil. Arrange 4 langoustines on the oiled wrap and fold over the unoiled half. Beat the 4 langoustines gently until paper thin. Repeat with the others. Place in the refrigerator to chill for 20 minutes.*

*Juice the oranges and lemon. Pour the juices into a small saucepan and boil for 8 minutes until reduced. Set aside to cool.*

# with Asparagus

Put the remaining olive oil, finely chopped tarragon, and coarse grain mustard into a small bowl, then beat in the cooled citrus juice to make a dressing. Season the dressing to taste with salt and pepper, and reserve it.

Just before serving, take the langoustine carpaccio out of the fridge and leave it to stand for a few minutes. Remove the plastic wrap and arrange the langoustine slices on a plate.

Cut the asparagus into 3 in/8 cm-long pieces. Check the seasoning in the dressing, adjust if necessary, and pour it over the langoustine slices. Arrange the asparagus decoratively on the plate. Garnish the langoustine slices with a sprig or two of fresh dill. Serve well chilled.

# Tuna with

Preparation time: 20 minutes
Cooking time: 15 minutes
Difficulty: ★

**Serves 4**

| | |
|---|---|
| 3 generous cups/500 g | zucchini |
| 2 cups/500 ml | chicken stock |
| ¾ cup/180 ml | olive oil |
| | salt |
| | pepper |
| ½ bunch | fresh chives |

| | |
|---|---|
| ½ bunch | fresh chervil |
| 1 sprig | fresh tarragon |
| 3½ tbsp/50g | capers |
| 1 | shallot |
| 12 oz/350 g | red tuna |
| 2 tbsp | olive oil |

**For the garnish:**

| | |
|---|---|
| 1 | leek |
| | rock salt |
| | oil for deep frying |

Zucchini take the lead in this recipe. They are very popular in Mediterranean countries, especially in the dish, ratatouille. This recipe by Francis Robin is particularly suitable as a refreshing appetizer in summer, because that's when zucchini have the best flavor. Zucchini is one of the oldest varieties of vegetable; it was in use in Mexico as early as the 8th century B.C.

Choose small, firm, dark green zucchini. If they do not seem to have a strong enough flavor for this recipe, you can add a crushed clove of garlic to heighten it. To retain the zucchini's attractive bright green color in the dressing, avoid using too much olive oil as it leaches out color.

The other key ingredient in our recipe is red tuna from the Mediterranean Sea. This big, meaty fish must be very fresh. It is available between May and September. At the end of the 19th century, lookouts drew the attention of

Provençal fishermen to shoals of tuna by blowing trumpets. If you cannot find fresh tuna, you could use fresh salmon, which will work just as well.

The tarragon used in this recipe intensifies the flavor of the tuna meat and enriches the dish with its own spicy-sweet aroma, but the dish will work just as well without this herb. The other fresh herbs, chervil and chives, are often used simply as a garnish. In our recipe, on the other hand, they have the important job of lending a special flavor to the tuna tartar.

*Wash the zucchini and cut them into chunks. Bring a pan of salted water to the boil, add the zucchini, and simmer for around 5–8 minutes, until they just start to soften.*

*Rinse the zucchini under cold running water and leave them to drain. Purée the zucchini using a food processor or hand blender, adding the chicken stock and olive oil. Season to taste with salt and pepper, and put aside.*

*Finely chop the chives, chervil, and tarragon. Drain the capers and chop them finely too, as well as the shallot.*

# Zucchini Cream

Dice the tuna very finely. Season with salt and pepper, and put aside. Brush 4 small ramekins or molds with a little olive oil.

In a bowl combine the diced tuna, chopped capers, shallot, and herbs with a little oil. Divide the tuna mixture between the molds, press it down well, and put in the refrigerator to chill. Wash the leek and slice a 2–2½ in/6 cm-long white piece into very thin strips.

Heat some oil in a pan and deep fry the leek until crisp and brown. Drain and reserve. Unmold the tuna tartar onto a plate. Pile some of the deep-fried leek on top of the tuna, and sprinkle over a few grains of rock salt. Pour the zucchini cream around the tuna. Serve chilled.

# Salad of Dried Salt Cod

Preparation time: 15 minutes
Fish soaking
      time: 24 hours
Cooking time: 55 minutes
Difficulty: ★

**Serves 4**

| | |
|---|---|
| 24 | pitted black olives |
| 2 | red bell peppers |
| 14 oz/400 g | dried salt cod fillet |

**For the vinaigrette:**

| | |
|---|---|
| 2 sprigs | fresh parsley |
| 2 | plum tomatoes |
| 1 | scallion |
| 2 cloves | garlic |
| 6 tbsp | olive oil |
| 1 tbsp | Banyuls vinegar (or balsamic vinegar) |
| | pepper |

In Catalan, finely diced or puréed cod is called *esqueixade*. In this recipe the cod is sliced thinly before being mixed with the other ingredients and vinegar. Our chef emphasizes the importance of attractive presentation in a dish. "*Esqueixade* was originally served with coarsely chopped olives. I prefer the olives to be so finely chopped, they look like breadcrumbs. Sprinkled over the fish, it gives this appetizer an attractive piquancy."

Dried salt cod, *morue* in French, *bacalao* in Catalan, is used in many recipes from the south of France, but these names apply only to cod from cold waters that has been salted and dried. When fresh, it is called *cabillaud* in French. You should always remember to soak the fish well and change the water several times.

In this appetizer, the meltingly tender *esquiexade* harmonizes beautifully with the crunchy chopped olives. When

this little oval fruit grows on the olive tree, it has a delicate green skin. As it gradually ripens, it first turns red, then purple, and finally black.

Banyuls vinegar lends a sweet note to the other ingredients. Because it is sold predominantly in Roussillon, in the south of France, it may be difficult to obtain, so here Monsieur Vila gives you the secret recipe. Mix one-third red wine vinegar with two-thirds Banyuls wine, then add a clove of garlic, a bay leaf, and a sprig of thyme. Leave the mixture to mature for 8–9 months. In the meantime you can use balsamic vinegar.

*Drain the olives. Chop them roughly, spread on a baking sheet, and bake in a preheated oven for around 40 minutes at 300 °F/150 °C.*

*Remove the olives from the oven, let them cool, then use a rolling pin to crush them to a black powder.*

*Turn up the oven to 400 °F/200 °C. Place the bell peppers on a baking sheet and bake them in the oven for 15 minutes. Let them cool, skin and deseed them, then spread the flesh out flat. Use a small round cutter to cut slices of bell pepper.*

# with Bell Peppers and Olives

Prepare the vinaigrette by combining the chopped parsley, diced tomatoes, finely chopped scallion and garlic, olive oil, and vinegar. Season to taste with pepper.

Drain the salt cod, pat it dry with kitchen paper, then slice it very thinly. Use the round cutter to cut out circles of cod. Reserve the fish trimmings.

Finely dice the fish trimmings and add them to the vinaigrette. Leave them to marinate for 5 minutes. Place a couple of spoonfuls of vinaigrette in the center of a plate. Arrange the circles of salt cod and bell pepper on top in a rosette shape, and sprinkle the crushed black olives on top.

# Collioure Anchovies

Preparation time: 1 hour
Marinating time: 2 hours
Cooking time: 30 minutes
Difficulty: ★

**Serves 4**

| 4 | red bell peppers |
| generous ¾ cup/ 200 ml | olive oil |
| 4 cloves | garlic |
| | salt |
| | pepper |
| 1 tbsp | chopped fresh parsley |
| 14 oz/400 g | salted anchovies |
| 1 | orange |

**For the herb salad:**

| 1 sprig | fresh basil |
| 4 sprigs | fresh cilantro |
| ¼ bunch | fresh chives |
| 4 sprigs | fresh flat-leaf parsley |
| 8 | fresh mint leaves |
| 1 handful | fresh baby spinach |
| 4 leaves | fresh sorrel (if available) |
| 4 sprigs | fresh chervil (8 if sorrel not used) |
| 1 bunch | scallions |
| 1 tbsp | Banyuls vinegar (or balsamic vinegar) |
| 2 tbsp | olive oil |

This colorful dish is child's play to prepare. Bell peppers, a typical Mediterranean vegetable, are at home just as much in France as in Italy. Christopher Columbus brought them with him from Cuba on his return to Spain at the end of the 15th century, and they were first cultivated in Spain.

Bell peppers are available in various colors: The ripe, red fruit are sweetest. Here they offset the salty taste of the anchovies. Like eggplant, bell peppers are a member of the nightshade family. You should only buy peppers that have a smooth, shiny skin. You should also ensure that the stalk is firmly attached to the pepper. Bell peppers will keep in your refrigerator's salad compartment for up to a week.

Here's a handy tip from Jean Plouzennec for skinning bell peppers. After baking the bell peppers in the oven, wrap them in aluminum foil. Let them cool down slowly, then unwrap them, and the skin will come away easily. Marinate the bell peppers in a good quality, strong, flavorful olive oil – extra-virgin oil is best.

To make life simple, use canned anchovies. If you buy the fish salted, though, and want to keep them, you must cover them well with a brine solution, otherwise they spoil very quickly. These little fish are easy to identify by their mouths. The jaw is disproportionately large and extends beyond the eyes. Anchovies are plentiful in the Mediterranean Sea area. They have been the basis for the international reputation of Collioure, a fishing village on France's Côte Vermeille, for hundreds of years. Thanks to its superb position, after the Peace of the Pyrenees in 1659 Collioure was exempt from the tax on salt. The French king recognized the importance of salt to Collioure's economy and decided not to tax it any more.

*A day before you want to eat the salad, heat the oven to 400 °F/200 °C for 15 minutes. Wash the bell peppers, drizzle with 1 tbsp olive oil, and bake for 30 minutes. Wrap them in foil and leave to cool. Skin the peppers, cut them open, deseed them, and cut the flesh into strips.*

*Place the strips of bell pepper on a plate. Peel 2 cloves garlic, thinly slice, and scatter over the peppers. Drizzle 8 tbsp olive oil over the peppers. Season them with salt and pepper, and sprinkle with 1 tbsp finely chopped parsley. Marinate for at least 2 hours.*

*The anchovies should be prepared in advance too. Place them in cold water for several hours, changing the water frequently. Drain them, pat them dry, and divide each into 2 fillets by pulling them apart, starting at the tail. Put the fillets on absorbent kitchen paper.*

# with Bell Peppers

Thinly slice the remaining cloves of garlic. Arrange the anchovy fillets on a plate and scatter the sliced garlic on top. Drizzle 8 tbsp olive oil over the anchovies. Do not add any salt. Leave the anchovies to marinate overnight.

Next day, arrange the strips of bell pepper on a plate in a fan shape. Place an anchovy fillet in between each strip of pepper. Peel the orange and cut into segments. Arrange the segments decoratively on the plate.

To make the herb salad: Strip the herb leaves from the stalks, cut the scallions into 1½ in/4 cm-long strips, and pick over the spinach. Combine the herbs, scallions, and spinach, dress with the vinegar and olive oil, and season to taste with salt and pepper.

# Anchovy Rosettes

Preparation time: 1 hour
Vinegar marinade: 1 hour
Olive oil marinade: 2 hours
Cooking time: 20 minutes
Difficulty: ★

**Serves 4**

| | |
|---|---|
| 1 lb/500 g | fresh anchovies |
| 5 | large potatoes |
| 4 | medium tomatoes |
| ½ cup/100 g | pitted black olives |
| 2 bulbs | fennel |
| | pepper |

**For the vinegar marinade:**
| | |
|---|---|
| 1 cup/250 ml | white vinegar |
| | rock salt |

**For the oil marinade:**
| | |
|---|---|
| 2 cloves | garlic |
| 1 bunch | fresh parsley |
| 1 bunch | fresh chives |
| 1 | lemon |
| 1 cup/250 ml | olive oil |

**For the garnish:**
| | |
|---|---|
| 7 oz/200 g | corn salad |

This delicious Mediterranean appetizer can also be served as a canapé with aperitifs. The anchovies, caught primarily between Sète and Collioure, are a maximum of 8 inches/ 20 centimeters long. They are sold fresh, whole, or as fillets in brine, but they are also available canned, preserved in oil. You could ask your fishmonger to fillet the anchovies for you, or our chef suggests you could marinate the fish whole.

It is worth preparing the marinade in advance, because the fresh anchovies are "cooked" during marinating. Sprinkle the fish with rock salt and turn them occasionally, so that they soak up the vinegar. You could also use tuna instead of anchovies, but this takes longer to marinate. Note that the anchovies have already been preserved in brine. Bear this in mind when you season the fennel purée. The olive oil marinade helps the ingredients to stay fresh much longer. Anchovies will keep in the refrigerator for up to one week.

You can always drain off the oil, reserve it, and use it to marinate more anchovies.

Fennel originates from Italy, but is cultivated in Provence and Spain. This aromatic plant, whose fat bulb consists of layers of fleshy leaves, is eaten as a vegetable or salad. Fennel is in season between October and May. It should be pale, firm, and round, with no brown marks.

The fennel purée is served cold. Sometimes Monsieur Yagues uses spinach or corn salad instead of fennel, and adds a few drops of oil from the marinade to the tomatoes and olives just before serving.

*Separate the anchovy fillets using the thumb and index finger, and rinse under cold, running water. Marinate them for 1 hour in the white vinegar and rock salt.*

*Wash and peel the potatoes. Slice them into ¼ in/5 mm-thick rounds and, using a serrated cookie cutter, cut out circles about 1¼ in/3 cm in diameter. Bring a pan of salted water to the boil, add the potatoes and simmer for 8 minutes. Drain the potato slices and leave them to cool.*

*Wash the tomatoes. Put them in a bowl, pour boiling water over them and leave them to stand for a few minutes. Drain them. Skin and deseed 2 of them. Finely dice the olives and tomatoes and then put aside.*

# with Fennel Purée

Wash the fennel and slice it into very thin strips. Bring a pan of salted water to the boil, add the fennel and simmer for approximately 15 minutes. Drain the fennel, crush it gently with the back of a spoon, and leave it to cool. Season sparingly with pepper.

Rinse the anchovy fillets under cold running water and leave to drain. Put them in a bowl with the finely sliced garlic, coarsely chopped parsley, finely chopped chives, and lemon slices. Pour over the olive oil and marinate for 2 hours. Drain the fillets, reserving the marinade.

Roughly chop the remaining 2 tomatoes and sweat in a frying pan. Roll the fillets around the tomatoes. Place each on a slice of potato and a corn salad leaf. Put a timbale of fennel purée in the middle of the plate. Sprinkle over the tomatoes and olives and drizzle with 1 tbsp marinade.

# Asparagus Salad

Preparation time:   30 minutes
Cooking time:   8–12 minutes
Difficulty:   ★

**Serves 4**

| 2¼ lb/1 kg | green asparagus |
| 1 tbsp | rock salt |
| 1½ cups/300 g | fresh fava beans |
| 2 | tomatoes |
| 1 bunch | fresh basil |

**For the balsamic vinaigrette:**
| 6 tbsp | olive oil |
| 2 tbsp | balsamic vinegar |
| | salt |
| | pepper |

**For the garnish:**
3½ oz/100 g parmesan

In Rouret, a village in the countryside around Nice, Daniel Ettlinger prepares dishes based on seasonal produce for his guests. Of course, asparagus is on his menu in spring. Ettlinger has a real weakness for this perennial plant and has created an appetizer based on asparagus that is named after his restaurant: asparagus salad "Clos Saint-Pierre."

When buying asparagus it should be firm, bright green and, when snapped in half, the stem should be shiny with juice. Monsieur Ettlinger suggests you try his favorite asparagus, purple, when it's in season. It's very delicate, but packed full of flavor. Regrettably this variety, which is mainly cultivated in the area around Nice, is seen on the market less and less. For some years it has been grown in glasshouses that retain the heat.

Our chef prefers not to prepare this dish using white asparagus. If he can't get hold of purple, he uses green asparagus, as is the case here. When preparing the asparagus, if the ends are a little dry, snap them off. The rock salt added to the cooking water helps the asparagus retain its bright green color. Be sure to refresh the asparagus in ice water after cooking, as explained in the method.

Tender little fava beans, also a French specialty, are a popular accompaniment to an aperitif. They are in season from May until the end of summer. The beans are eaten with the skin on.

Basil is a highly aromatic kitchen herb that gives a distinctive flavor to this appetizer.

*Wash the asparagus and scrape off the scales on the stalk. Peel the asparagus stalks from top to bottom using a vegetable peeler.*

*Bring a saucepan with 6 cups/1.5 l water and 1 tbsp rock salt to the boil. Add the asparagus and simmer for 8–12 minutes, depending on the thickness of the stalks. Drain, and plunge into a bowl of ice water for 10 minutes. Drain again, and place on kitchen paper.*

*Shell the fava beans. Cook in 2 cups boiling water for 5 minutes, drain and reserve. Put the tomatoes in a bowl, pour boiling water over them, and leave for 1 minute. Drain, skin and deseed the tomatoes. Cut the flesh into thick strips. Wash the basil and finely chop the leaves.*

# "Clos Saint-Pierre"

To make the vinaigrette, put the balsamic vinegar and olive oil in a bowl, add salt and pepper to taste, then beat well.

Add the fava beans, chopped tomatoes, and basil to the vinaigrette.

Cut the asparagus into finger-length pieces and arrange them on a plate in a criss-cross pattern. Drizzle generously with the vinaigrette. Arrange the tomatoes, fava beans, and basil around the asparagus. Garnish with a few shavings of parmesan.

# "Côte d' Azur" Salad with

| | |
|---|---|
| Preparation time: | 30 minutes |
| Cooking time: | 15 minutes |
| Difficulty: | ☆ |

**Serves 4**

| | |
|---|---|
| 1 | small eggplant |
| 2 | zucchini |
| 2 cloves | garlic |
| 5 tbsp | olive oil |
| | salt, pepper |
| 2 sprigs | fresh basil |
| | leaves from 4 stalks celery |
| 3–4/20 g | scallions |
| 6 | fresh peppermint leaves |
| 1 sprig | fresh thyme |

| | |
|---|---|
| 2 | red bell peppers |
| 1½ oz/40 g | Reggiano parmesan (5 years old) |

| | |
|---|---|
| 1 | tomato |
| 1 cup/80 g | mesclun |

**For the balsamic vinaigrette:**

| | |
|---|---|
| 4 tbsp | olive oil |
| 4 tbsp | balsamic vinegar |
| 4 tbsp | wine vinegar |
| 1 tbsp | candied stem ginger syrup (optional) |
| ½ tsp | salt |
| 1 pinch | pepper |

**For the garnish:**

| | |
|---|---|
| ¼ cup/30 g | black olives |
| 1 small sprig | fresh lemon thyme (optional) |

This salad is a wonderful appetizer from the south that makes the most of eggplant, zucchini, and especially basil. Basil originates from India and its name comes from the Greek *basilikos*, meaning "royal." This is a clear indication of the importance attached to this herb in antiquity.

Basil gives off a strong scent, reminiscent of lemon and jasmine. Basil that has wilted comes alive again if it is plunged into water for a moment, but not for too long, otherwise the leaves turn dark. For our recipe, pinch the top two leaves from each sprig to use as a garnish.

Our chef mainly uses 5-year-old parmesan, because the older it is, the stronger the flavor. Sautéing the vegetables in hot oil is critical to the success of this dish.

Here's another tip from the professionals: To make it easier to remove the skin from bell peppers, after baking them in

the oven, wrap them in newspaper or aluminum foil for 3–4 minutes. The garlic should be blanched well to lessen the strong flavor. To do this, peel the cloves, immerse them in cold water, and then in boiling water. Repeat this process three times.

Peppermint is characterized by its small, long leaves with blackish graining. You can substitute ordinary mint for peppermint, and use ordinary thyme if you can't find lemon thyme.

When preparing the balsamic vinaigrette, add a tablespoon of water to prevent the mixture from separating. Ginger syrup is not absolutely necessary, but the sweet and sour flavor lends a very special note to the dressing.

*Wash the eggplant and zucchini. Slice them very thinly. Peel the garlic, slice it very thinly, and blanch it by first immersing it in cold water, then in boiling water. Repeat this process 3 times.*

*Heat the olive oil in a pan and sauté the sliced eggplant and zucchini for 1 minute. Drain the vegetables, season with salt and pepper, and reserve.*

*Pinch off the top leaves from the sprigs of basil, and the tender green leaves from the celery sticks, reserving them for the garnish. Finely chop 2 large basil leaves, the scallions, and peppermint. Strip the leaves from the sprig of thyme. Add the herbs to the vegetables.*

# Balsamic Vinegar Dressing

Lightly oil a baking sheet, place the bell peppers on it, and broil them for about 10 minutes. When the peppers have cooled, skin and deseed them, then chop them into thin strips. Reserve the chopped peppers.

Using a vegetable peeler, shave off long strips from the parmesan. Wash the tomato, put in a bowl and pour boiling water over it to blanch it. Leave it for a few minutes, drain, then skin and deseed. Dice the tomato flesh.

Balsamic vinaigrette: Beat together the olive oil, balsamic vinegar, wine vinegar, ginger syrup, salt, and pepper. Toss the salad ingredients with the dressing. Garnish with mesclun, the reserved sprigs of basil and celery, olives, lemon thyme (if used), and parmesan shavings.

# Marinated

Preparation time:   25 minutes
Difficulty:   ★

**Serves 4**

| | |
|---|---|
| 3½ lb/1.5 kg | sardines |
| | salt |
| | pepper |
| 1 cup/250 ml | white wine vinegar |
| 1 clove | garlic |
| 1 | onion |

| | |
|---|---|
| 6 sprigs | fresh thyme |
| 2 | bay leaves |
| | juice of 2 lemons |
| | Tabasco sauce to taste |
| 1 cup/250 ml | olive oil |

**For the garnish:**

| | |
|---|---|
| 4 | cherry tomatoes |
| | fresh thyme |
| | bay leaves |

In days gone by, millions of sardines caused the water in Marseilles' Old Port to shimmer. According to folklore, a sardine is supposed to have once barred the entrance to this important place. Obviously it wasn't one of the small in size rainbow-hued relatives of the herring that entered into folklore, but a ship called La Sardine. But these fish can be found on quayside stalls in Marseilles.

They are at their most delicious in spring. These delicate, silvery-blue fish need very careful treatment. They must be chilled immediately, but not for too long, or they spoil. Meaty sardines are the best and are caught using the traditional *lamparo* method. The fishermen attach a bright light to the prow of their boat, attracting the fish into their nets.

Look for very fresh sardines with shiny scales, bright eyes, and very red gills. To fillet the fish, first you have to slit

them open from the gills down. Then slide a knife blade down along the spine.

Because these fish are very rich, Jean-Michel Minguella likes to marinate them in lemon juice. They should not be served with a heavy, rich sauce, which would overpower the flavor of the sardines. It's best to use a high-quality regional olive oil from the first pressing that is an extra-virgin oil, to season the raw sardines, which are "cold cured" by the vinegar. A very aromatic oil is especially suitable.

The garlic should also be of an excellent quality. It should be aromatic, the bulbs firm and unblemished. Use the Tabasco sauce sparingly. It should not color the dish.

*Scale and clean the sardines. Ensure that the fish don't fall apart when you are scaling them. Remove the backbones too.*

*Fillet the fish by running the tip of a knife lengthwise through the middle, starting beneath the gills. Season with salt and pepper to taste.*

*Lay the sardine fillets in a dish, pour over the white wine vinegar, and leave them to marinate for a few minutes. Drain the fish as soon as they turn a lighter color, and put them aside.*

# Sardines

Peel the garlic and onion, and slice them thinly. Strip the thyme leaves and chop the bay leaves. Mix the herbs together. Juice the lemons.

Lay the sardine fillets in a dish. Scatter the onion and garlic over them, then the herbs. Season them with a dash or two of Tabasco and the lemon juice.

Season the sardines with salt. Pour the olive oil over them, then refrigerate them. To serve, spoon the marinade onto the plate, then arrange the sardine fillets on top in a star shape. Garnish with the cherry tomatoes, sprigs of thyme, and bay leaves.

# Tomato Surprise

Preparation time: 30 minutes
Cooking time: 15 minutes
Difficulty: ★

**Serves 4**

| | |
|---|---|
| 4 | beefsteak tomatoes, each around 6 oz/180 g |
| 8 | langoustines |
| 3 tbsp | olive oil |
| ⅓ cup + 1½ tbsp/ 100 ml | chicken stock |
| 1 clove | garlic |
| 12 oz/350 g | soft goat milk cheese |

| | |
|---|---|
| 1 bunch | fresh chives |
| 3½ tbsp/80 g | black olive paste (or *tapenade*) |
| | mixed salad |

**For the balsamic vinaigrette:**

| | |
|---|---|
| | juice of ½ lemon |
| 1 tbsp | olive oil |
| 1 tsp | balsamic vinegar |
| | salt |
| | pepper |

In this dish Joël Garault has taken his inspiration from the Provençal countryside. Originally farmers stored fresh goat milk cheese, seasoned with chives, wild arugula, olive oil, and pepper, under an olive tree. In fact this summery starter with langoustines pays homage to regional cuisine.

Tomatoes are important in this dish. The most suitable are round, red *Marmande* tomatoes which are available from July to October. The tomatoes should be firm, meaty, shiny and evenly colored.

Before scooping out the flesh, make an incision on three sides of the tomato, so it retains its attractive shape.

The surprise is the soft goat milk cheese filling. Made solely from goat's milk, this cheese contains a minimum of 45 percent fat. Ask for a *Billy* from the Tarn or a cheese from the Cher department. The cheese must be at peak freshness.

The black olive paste, for which you can use *tapenade* if necessary, is also an unusual ingredient.

You can prepare the tomatoes the day before, but the langoustines should be prepared at the last minute. This tasty, pink-shelled crustacean is available from April to August. When buying, ensure that the shell is shiny, and the eyes bright black. After shelling, the digestive tract must be removed. Joël Garault inserts a wooden toothpick into each langoustine to prevent it from curling up during cooking. Don't forget to remove the toothpick before serving.

Pour boiling water over the tomatoes in a bowl and leave for a few minutes. Drain and skin. Slice the top off each tomato, scoop out the flesh, and reserve. Place the tomatoes upside down on absorbent kitchen paper to drain the juices. Cut the tops to form a fan for the garnish.

Shell the langoustines, reserving the heads and shells for the sauce. Heat 1 tbsp olive oil in a frying pan and sauté the langoustines until golden brown. Season to taste with salt and pepper and put aside.

To make the sauce, put the langoustine heads and shells in a saucepan with the chicken stock. Crush them with a spatula. Add 1 tbsp olive oil, the chopped garlic, and tomato flesh to the chicken stock, bring to the boil, and simmer for around 5 minutes.

# with Langoustines

Strain the sauce, beat it well with a wire whisk, and add the lemon juice, olive oil, and balsamic vinegar. Season to taste with salt and pepper, and leave to cool.

To make the filling, mash the goat milk cheese with 1 tbsp olive oil. Finely chop the chives, reserving the tips for the garnish. Stir the chopped chives into the cheese.

Stuff half of each tomato with the cheese mixture, add a layer of olive paste, then finish with more cheese. Slice each langoustine in half lengthwise. Arrange the mixed salad, langoustines, and tomato (showing the filling) on each plate. Garnish with chives, tomato fans, and sauce.

# Hot Appetizers

# Red Mullet with

Preparation time: 30 minutes
Cooking time: 15 minutes
Difficulty: ★★

**Serves 4**

| | |
|---|---|
| 4 | baby globe artichokes |
| | juice of 1 lemon |
| 1 | medium potato |
| | salt |
| 1 pinch | saffron |
| 4 | pitted black olives |
| 6 | red mullet, |
| | each 5 oz/150 g |
| ⅓ cup + 1½ tbsp/ | |
| 100 ml | olive oil |

| | |
|---|---|
| 6½ tbsp/100 g | black olive paste |
| 1 cup/100 g | mixed salad |
| 1 handful | fresh chives |

**For the mayonnaise:**

| | |
|---|---|
| 1 | egg yolk |
| ⅓ cup + 1½ tbsp/ | |
| 100 ml | peanut oil |
| 1 tsp | wine vinegar |
| | juice of 1 lemon |
| | salt |
| | pepper |

**For the balsamic vinaigrette:**

| | |
|---|---|
| 1 tbsp | olive oil |
| 1 tsp | balsamic vinegar |
| | salt |
| | pepper |

Here's an appetizer recipe from the south of France that announces the arrival of spring, because that's the time of year that red mullet start to arrive on the Côte d'Azur. These fish are especially prized for their delicate flesh and unique flavor. If it is difficult to obtain red mullet, red snapper can be used instead.

If you don't want to fillet the fish yourself, ask your fish-monger to do it for you. It's important to ensure that all the bones are removed. You may be able to buy small mackerel, which you can use instead. A tip from our chef: When baking the fish fillets, cover with aluminum foil to prevent the smell transferring to the oven.

For this recipe you need baby globe artichokes, *poivrades* in French, which are easily identified by their coloring. The purple parts gradually turn into attractive spikes.

When they are young they can be eaten raw. The leaves must be intact, unblemished, and tightly closed.

Place the hearts in water with lemon juice added, so they do not discolor. As soon as they are sliced they must be mixed with the mayonnaise and lemon juice. You can use ready-made mayonnaise; you just need a teaspoonful to bind the ingredients. Depending on the time of year, our chef adds tender young fava beans to the dish.

If the mayonnaise seems too thick, add a little of the cooking water from the potato. The saffron-infused water will lend a delicate hint of flavor to the mayonnaise.

The olive paste gives the fish a fruity taste. Dry the sliced olives on kitchen paper.

*Starting at the base, cut off the artichoke leaves. Leave a little of the stalk attached to the heart. Place the artichoke hearts in water acidulated with lemon. Then remove the choke with the tip of a spoon.*

*Cut the artichoke hearts into strips, then put them back in the acidulated water. Peel the potato and slice it into rounds. Boil a pan of salted water, add the saffron and sliced potato (you could use a cutter for these), and simmer for 10 minutes. Drain the potato, reserving the liquid.*

*Beat together the mayonnaise ingredients, and add the juice of 1 lemon. If the mayonnaise seems too thick, add a little cooking liquid from the potato. Carefully toss the artichoke slices in the mayonnaise, then put them aside. Slice the black olives into rings and leave to drain.*

# Artichoke Hearts

Scale the red mullet, fillet them, and remove the bones with a pair of tweezers. Place 6 fillets skin side up on a plate, and drizzle the olive oil over them.

Spread the black olive paste over the skin side of the remaining fillets, reserving some for assembling the dish. Broil all the fillets for 5 minutes at 320 °F/160 °C. Wash the salad and prepare the balsamic vinaigrette by beating together all the ingredients.

Place a circle of black olive paste on top of each potato. Arrange the artichoke slices on the plate in a fan shape and garnish them with the olive rings. Place 3 fillets, 1 slice of potato, and a handful of salad, garnished with chives and dressed with vinaigrette, on each plate.

# Cod Purée with

| Preparation time: | 40 minutes |
| Fish soaking time: | 24 hours |
| Cooking time: | 30 minutes |
| Difficulty: | ★ |

**Serves 4**

| 10 oz/300 g | dried salt cod |
| 10 oz/300 g | fresh cod |
| 2 cups/500 ml | milk |
| | zest of 1 orange, unwaxed |
| ½–1 oz/10 g | fresh root ginger (optional) |
| 3 tbsp | olive oil |
| 4 cloves | garlic |

| | salt |
| | pepper |
| ½ | baguette |

**For the garlic cream:**

| ½ bulb | garlic |
| 1 cup/250 ml | milk |
| 1 cup/250 ml | light cream |
| | salt |
| | pepper |

**For the garnish:**

| 2 oz/50 g | black truffle |
| | ground paprika (optional) |

In Nîmes, cod purée is just as important as the Roman amphitheatres, the ancient Maison Carée, or public holidays. This cold-water fish is known as *morue* when it is salted or dried. Fresh, it is called *cabillaud*.

For this recipe it is important to soak the fish thoroughly, to remove as much of the salt as possible. The water should be changed several times. Before using the fish in the recipe, remove the skin and bones. When cooked in milk the fish takes on a pale color.

Christian Étienne uses garlic in all his recipes, and this one is no exception. Garlic originated in Central Asia and is a member of the lily family.

To lessen the intensity of the flavor, the garlic is blanched several times in boiling milk and cold water. Only then should it be added to the sauce.

The orange zest gives a hint of this dish's Provençal origins. The same applies to the ginger, but this ingredient is optional.

The cod purée, or *brandade* as it is known in France, is served hot. The Vaucluse truffle garnish is an elegant touch. Truffles are available in widely varying sizes (you may have to go to a specialty shop for them). They are mostly black or dark brown, but some are gray, or even white. If you want to serve a more rustic dish, dispense with the truffle and use roughly chopped black olives instead. Finish off with a garnish of thyme.

*Chop the fresh cod and well-soaked salt cod into large chunks. In a saucepan, bring the milk to the boil; add the orange zest, grated root ginger (if using), and fish. Poach the fish in the milk for around 3–4 minutes.*

*Drain the fish and transfer it to a heavy-based pan. Mash it with a spatula until it forms a purée.*

*Heat the pan on low heat. Add a thin trickle of olive oil, beating the fish purée hard with a wooden spoon. Continue heating for 15 minutes, until it forms a smooth mixture.*

# Black Truffle Slivers

Peel the 4 garlic cloves and crush them with the back of a fork. Fold the garlic into the cod pureé. Season the purée to taste with salt and pepper, but be sparing with the salt. Keep the purée warm.

Garlic cream: Bring the milk to the boil, blanch 3 peeled garlic cloves in the milk, then plunge them into cold water. Repeat 3 times. Stir the blanched garlic into the cream in a saucepan, then heat gently to the boil, and simmer for 20 minutes. Purée in a blender, and season to taste.

Toast slices of baguette in the oven for 3 minutes. Rub the toasted bread with a piece of garlic. Arrange 3 tbsp cod purée in the center of the plate and top with slivers of truffle. Pour a little garlic cream around the fish, sprinkle with ground paprika, and serve with the toast.

# Stuffed Squid

Preparation time: 35 minutes
Cooking time: 20 minutes
Difficulty: ★

**Serves 4**

| | |
|---|---|
| 4 | small squid, each 4 oz/100 g |
| | salt |
| | pepper |
| 2 tbsp | olive oil |
| 1 | onion |
| 2 cloves | garlic |
| 1 | red bell pepper |

| | |
|---|---|
| 3½ tbsp/50 g | pitted black olives |
| ½ bunch | fresh parsley |
| 2 oz/50 g | purslane (or other small, mild salad leaves) |

**For the balsamic vinaigrette:**

| | |
|---|---|
| 1 tbsp | balsamic vinegar |
| 3 tbsp | olive oil |
| 4 tsp/20 g | puréed tomatoes |
| ½ bunch | chives |
| 2 tsp/10 g | chopped fresh tarragon |
| 4 tsp/20 g | puréed tomatoes |
| | salt |
| | pepper |

With this appetizer our chef pays homage to his mother. It was she who taught him the flavors of Provençal food, and this appetizer is a reminder of his childhood. It gives Christian Étienne great pleasure to recall this dish being prepared at home: "My brother and I always fought over who should prepare the squid. I loved helping my mother when she put together this dish."

Squid, or calamari, is a mollusk, a member of the cephalopod family. It is extremely popular throughout the Mediterranean. When cleaning the squid, ensure that the bodies remain whole and, in this recipe, remember to remove the toothpicks before serving.

The red bell pepper gives the stuffing a fruity flavor. This vegetable is a member of the nightshade family and is a versatile vegetable that differs from other varieties of pepper, mainly because of its size and mild flavor. When you buy bell peppers, the skin should be shiny. The seeds, and often the skin, are removed before bell peppers are used in cooking. Our chef blanches the bell pepper in boiling water for about ten minutes, to make the flavor milder, and then refreshes it in cold water. You could use a little ratatouille of eggplant and zucchini to stuff the squid, instead of bell pepper.

Purslane is a hardy salad that originates from India. It was highly prized by the Romans for its piquant taste. This magnesium-rich plant is mainly eaten as a salad.

Mamie Simone's recipe bears the hallmarks of the Sète region. It's an easy to prepare, refreshing appetizer that is eaten in the south of France mainly in summer.

*Prepare the squid by pulling off the head with tentacles from the body. Reserve the tentacles but discard the head. Reaching into the body, pull out the cartilage, or quill, being careful not to pierce the ink sac as you take it out. Peel the skin from the body. Rinse the squid well.*

*Season the squid with salt and pepper. Chop the tentacles very finely. Heat 1 tbsp olive oil in a skillet and sauté the chopped squid for 1 minute, until browned.*

*Add the finely chopped onion, and finely chopped garlic, and brown them, stirring occasionally.*

# à la Mamie

Wash the bell pepper and dice it finely. Bring a pan of salted water to the boil and blanch the diced pepper in it for about 10 minutes. Add the diced bell pepper, 7 tsp/35 g chopped black olives, and the chopped parsley to the squid, stir well, and season to taste.

Stuff each of the squid bodies with the stuffing mix until three-quarters full. Secure the ends of the squid with a toothpick. Heat the remaining olive oil in a skillet, and sauté the squid for 2–3 minutes until lightly browned.

Beat together the salt, pepper, vinegar, and oil to form a vinaigrette. Add the remaining black olives, puréed tomatoes, chopped chives and tarragon. Place a few purslane leaves, or salad leaves, in the center of the plate, arrange the squid around them, and top with the vinaigrette.

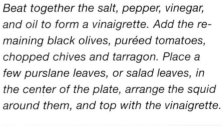

# Artichoke Hearts

Preparation time: 40 minutes
Cooking time: 25 minutes
Difficulty: ★★

**Serves 4**

| 16 | globe artichokes |
| 1 | lemon |

**For the vegetable accompaniment:**

| 2 | carrots |
| 2 | onions |
| 2 cloves | garlic |
| 1 tbsp | olive oil |
| 1 cup/250 ml | dry white wine |
| 1 | chicken bouillon cube |

**For the bouquet garni:**

| 1 | bay leaf |
| 2 sprigs each | fresh thyme, parsley |
| | salt, pepper |

**For the squid:**

| 1¼ lb/600 g | baby squid (or very small cuttlefish) |
| ⅛ stick/10 g | butter |
| 1 tbsp | olive oil |

**For the parsley butter:**

| ¼ stick/20 g | butter |
| 1 bunch | fresh parsley |
| 2 cloves | garlic |
| 1 tsp | Pernod (or other aniseed drink) |
| | salt, pepper |

**For the garnish:**

| | fresh chervil |

It was Catherine de Médicis, a definite gourmet, who introduced globe artichokes to France. Without them, our chef, Alain Carro, would not have been able to create this dish. In the process he was inspired by the artichoke creations of famous chef Roger Vergé, who lives in Mougins, near Cannes. In this area, globe artichokes are also referred to as "spiny," and the variety is known as *poivrades*. They are cultivated in the Var region, around Hyères, not far from our chef's restaurant.

A good artichoke must feel quite heavy, and firm, with hard, tight-packed leaves. They can be stored in your refrigerator's salad compartment for a few days. Note that as soon as they are cooked, they oxidize very quickly, so they are best served immediately after cooking. The purple, Provençal globe artichokes in our recipe have elongated heads, and are green, with purple shading in places.

This vegetable from the thistle family is rich in iron, and is a diuretic.

When prepared, the artichokes in this dish are reminiscent of mushrooms. In rural Provençal cuisine, artichokes are sometimes prepared in the same way as *barigoules*, which belong to the milk-cap family of mushrooms – they are cut off just below the head, drizzled with oil, and broiled.

Cuttlefish is very similar to squid. In southern France, small cuttlefish are called *pistes* or *supions*. This dish incorporates another Mediterranean specialty – *pastis*. In our recipe the skillet is deglazed with Pernod. If you can't obtain baby squid or very small cuttlefish, use the top part of an ordinary squid instead. In this dish Alain Carro succeeds perfectly in combining the aniseed flavor of the Pernod with the flavor of the artichokes.

Pull or cut the leaves off the artichokes. Use only the heart and the upper part of the stalk. Put the artichokes into water acidulated with lemon, so that they don't discolor.

Heat the butter and olive oil in a skillet. Sauté the cleaned and prepared baby squid (or small cuttlefish) for 1–2 minutes, until they are firm. All the liquid from them must evaporate. Drain the squid and put them aside.

Peel the carrots, then score grooves in them lengthwise. Slice them thinly. Peel and thinly slice the onions. Peel and slice the garlic. Heat the olive oil in a skillet. Sauté the vegetables and the bouquet garni herbs for a few minutes in the hot oil. Season with salt and pepper.

# with Squid

Drain the artichokes and add them to the pan with the vegetables. Sauté until the vegetables are golden brown. Sweat the vegetables on low heat for 15 minutes.

Deglaze the skillet with the white wine, and braise the vegetables for 5 minutes. Add the bouillon cube and stir until it has dissolved.

Mix the butter with the chopped parsley and finely chopped garlic, then add the Pernod. Add this parsley butter to the squid. Deglaze the pan with the Pernod. Season the squid to taste with salt and pepper, arrange on a plate, and garnish with a little chervil.

# Eggplant Stacks

Preparation time: 25 minutes
Salting time
    for eggplant: 1 hour
Cooking time: 20 minutes
Difficulty: ☆

**Serves 4**

| | |
|---|---|
| 2 | large eggplants |
| 6½ tbsp/100 g | rock salt |
| scant ½ cup/50 g | flour |
| ⅔ cup/150 ml | olive oil |
| 2 oz/50 g | mozzarella |
| 1 tbsp | chopped thyme |
| | salt |
| | pepper |

| | |
|---|---|
| ¼ cup/50 g | diced tomatoes |
| | freshly grated parmesan |
| 4 oz/100 g | wild arugula |

**For the balsamic vinaigrette:**

| | |
|---|---|
| 4 tbsp | olive oil |
| 1 tbsp | balsamic vinegar |
| 1 tbsp | wine vinegar |
| 1 tbsp | syrup from candied ginger |
| ½ tsp | salt |
| 1 pinch | pepper |

**For the garnish/assembly:**

| | |
|---|---|
| 2 cloves | garlic |
| 4 slices | air-dried ham |
| 4 tsp/20 g | black truffle slivers |
| 4 tsp/20 g | thin slivers parmesan |
| | rock salt |
| 4 sprigs | fresh thyme |
| | olive oil for frying |

This appetizer gets its name from the famous building in Nice where Laurent Broussier presides as head chef. The historic building that was once home to author and poet Maurice Maeterlinck lies between Nice and the road from Villefranche. In this quite exceptional setting, our chef, Laurent Broussier, creates elegant recipes for his customers, using exclusively Provençal ingredients.

Eggplant takes pride of place in this recipe. Originating from India, these long or round fruit first reached southern France in the 17th century. The Parisians didn't discover them until the time of the French Revolution! The smooth, shiny, purple to black skin of the eggplant (white eggplant is available too) encases pale, firm flesh. Originally, eggplant were cooked whole, larded, stuffed, or puréed. Our chef has dreamt up something different. For this recipe they are sliced, sautéed, and then baked with mozzarella. Line the baking sheet with aluminum foil, so that the

eggplant slices don't stick. To prevent the eggplant soaking up oil, remove it from the skillet as soon as it is cooked.

Nice is just a few miles from the Italian border, so it's hardly surprising that this appetizer uses mozzarella. This cheese is made in Lazio or Campania from buffalo's or cow's milk. Mozzarella is available in balls or slabs, in a variety of sizes. It is preserved in brine or whey.

Wild arugula, which grows on the Côte d'Azur, can be replaced by the less acidic cultivated arugula, or alternatively by curly endive.

*Wash the eggplants, pat them dry, and slice them into rounds. Place the slices in a dish, sprinkle rock salt over them, and leave them for 1 hour.*

*Rinse the eggplant slices and pat them dry. Toss them in the flour until well coated. Heat the olive oil in a skillet, sauté the eggplant for 2–3 minutes each side until golden brown, then keep warm.*

*Chop the mozzarella into small pieces, purée it in a food processor, adding the thyme, and salt and pepper to taste.*

# "Maeterlinck"

Take a slice of eggplant and put a layer of mozzarella purée on top, then add some of the diced tomato. Repeat until there are 3 layers of eggplant, then sprinkle each stack with grated parmesan. Place on a baking sheet, and bake in the oven for 12 minutes at 350 °F/180 °C.

Prepare the balsamic vinaigrette to dress the arugula by beating together the ingredients. Peel and slice the garlic. Blanch the garlic and sauté it in the oil. Coat the arugula in the dressing.

Wrap a slice of ham around each eggplant stack. Arrange a heap of arugula on the plate, next to the eggplant. Arrange the fried garlic slices, truffle and parmesan slivers, a few grains of rock salt, and a sprig of thyme on top of each of the eggplant stacks.

# Lentils and

Preparation time:   35 minutes
Cooking time:   35 minutes
Difficulty:   ★

**Serves 4**

| | |
|---|---|
| 2 | oranges |
| 2 | grapefruits |
| ½ | lemon |
| ¾ cup/150 g | Puy or green lentils |
| 1 clove | garlic, unpeeled and sliced in half |
| 1 sprig | fresh thyme |
| 1 | bay leaf |
| ⅓ cup + 1½ tbsp/ 100 ml | olive oil |

| | |
|---|---|
| | salt |
| 1 | shallot |
| 1 bunch | fresh chives |
| 12 | scallops |
| 6 slices | Parma ham |
| 1 bunch | wild arugula |

**For the vinaigrette:**

| | |
|---|---|
| 2 tbsp | olive oil |
| 1 | grapefruit segment |
| | lentil liquor |

**For the garnish:**

| | |
|---|---|
| 8 | orange segments |
| 4 | grapefruit segments |
| | fresh chives |

Lentils with scallops and citrus fruit is a fabulous combination! Joël Garault lightens this wintry appetizer with citrus fruit from the area around Menton.

As soon as the lentils start to cook, the grapefruit and lemon give off their slightly acidic aroma. Although citrus fruit are available throughout the year, their main season is November to March. Oranges are especially prized for their high vitamin C and vitamin A content. Depending on the variety, they can be sweet or sour, and more or less perfumed. Look for firm fruit with a smooth skin.

The grapefruit are also rich in these vitamins. Grapefruit vary in sweetness, depending on the color, the palest being the sharpest. If you prefer, the grapefruit can be omitted from this recipe. Lemons are also very rich in vitamin C. Look for very firm, unblemished fruit.

Our chef recommends buying little, green Puy lentils, which is a protected brand name. They grow on the volcanic soil of the Auvergne and benefit from the microclimate there. The dried lentils are not floury. They have a soft skin and delicate flavor. You should only add salt to lentils halfway through the cooking time, to prevent them turning hard.

When you buy the scallops, they should be closed. If they don't close when touched, they are not safe to eat. You can also prepare this appetizer using squid. Because the Parma ham is very salty, season the dish with salt sparingly.

*Juice 1 orange, 1 grapefruit, and ½ lemon. Put the lentils into a saucepan. Add the citrus juice, garlic, thyme, and bay leaf. Pour 1¾ cups/450 ml water into the pan with 1 tbsp olive oil. Bring to the boil and simmer for 30 minutes. Season to taste with salt after 15 minutes.*

*Drain the lentils, reserving the liquor. Fold the chopped shallot and finely chopped chives into the lentils. Open the scallops. Run a finger under the black beard and remove the meat from the shell. Wash the scallops and drain them.*

*Peel the remaining orange and grapefruit. Cut out 8 orange segments and 4 grapefruit segments for the garnish. Reserve an additional grapefruit segment for the vinaigrette.*

# Scallops

Juice what is left of the orange and grapefruit. Put 1 tbsp lentil liquor and 1 grapefruit segment in a bowl. Add 2 tbsp olive oil, and purée with a hand blender to form a dressing. Spoon 4 tbsp of this vinaigrette over the lentils.

Cut the Parma ham in half lengthwise and wrap a strip around each scallop. Secure the ham with a toothpick.

Sauté the scallops in olive oil for 1 minute on each side. Make a pile of lentils in the center of the plate. Garnish with orange, grapefruit, and chives. Cut each scallop into 2 slices, and arrange the slices around the lentils. Add arugula leaves with a little dressing.

# Braised Snails

Preparation time: 20 minutes
Cooking time: 1 hour 10 minutes
Difficulty: ☆

Serves 4

| 4 dozen | snails |
|---|---|
| 14 oz/400 g | squid |
| 1 tbsp | olive oil |
| | rock salt |
| 2 | tomatoes |
| 1 pinch | saffron |
| | table salt |
| | pepper |

**For the sofregit sauce:**

| 1 | onion |
|---|---|
| 1 clove | garlic |
| 5 oz/150 g | ground pork or beef |
| 1 tbsp | olive oil |

**For the bouquet garni:**

fresh thyme
bay leaf
fresh rosemary

In this recipe Jean Plouzennec introduces you to a typical Catalan dish. His mixture of flavors from field and sea is a clear indication that he's at home in the French department of Pyrénées-Orientales. This is also evident from the fact that he has prepared *sofregit*, a pillar of Catalan cuisine. This is a kind of basic sauce, with the ingredients varying according to personal taste. Over the border in Spain, it is known as *el sofrito*. Spain is able to offer another strange ingredient from the sea, the sea cucumber.

Catalonia is often very humid, and this is why the *petit gris* snails, or *escargots*, which are plentiful, are used in this dish. Gathering snails is carefully regulated in France. They taste best in winter, after they have fasted, because the meat is more tender and the flavor less acidic.

We recommend you to use prepared snails. If you buy fresh ones, it is very important that you follow the correct procedure before you include them in this recipe. We have not given the instructions for that here; you will need to consult other sources.

The marine element comes from the white flesh of the squid. If you are using whole squid, slice them in half or into rings. It is possible to buy deep-frozen squid, but it is best to use fresh, as the texture is better. If you are put off by the appearance of squid, ask your fishmonger to prepare them for you. The best season to eat squid is in the early fall.

*Try to obtain prepared snails for this recipe.*

*Prepare the squid by removing the head, the cartilage (quill), and ink sac. Peel the skin, rinse the squid, then squeeze gently to drain out some of the liquid. If too big, cut in half. Cut the squid into rings.*

*To make the sofregit, peel and chop the onion and garlic. Heat the olive oil in a large saucepan, and fry the onion and garlic. Add the ground beef or pork, and bouquet garni herbs, and fry them for 5 minutes. Remove the bouquet garni.*

# and Squid

Heat 1 tbsp olive oil in a skillet until very hot. Fry the squid until golden. Add a pinch of rock salt. Add the squid to the sofregit sauce and simmer for 2 minutes.

Put the tomatoes into a bowl. Pour over boiling water and remove them after a few minutes. Skin and deseed the tomatoes, dice finely and add to the squid mixture. Sprinkle the saffron over the squid. Season with salt and pepper, and simmer for 30 minutes on low heat.

Add the snails, cover the pan, and simmer the snails for another 30 minutes. Serve individual portions in mini casserole dishes.

# Fillet of Red Mullet

Preparation time: 1 hour
Cooking time: 20 minutes
Difficulty: ★★

**Serves 4**

| | |
|---|---|
| 6 | red mullet, each 5 oz/150 g |
| 2 | red potatoes (Desirée) |
| 3 tbsp | olive oil |
| 4 cloves | garlic |
| 3½ tbsp/50 g | black olive paste (or *tapenade*) |

| | |
|---|---|
| 2 | tomatoes |
| generous ¾ cup/ 200 ml | fish or chicken stock |
| ½ | lemon |
| 1 bunch | fresh parsley |
| | salt |
| | pepper |

**For the salad:**

| | |
|---|---|
| 3½ oz/100 g | arugula |
| 3½ oz/100 g | oak leaf lettuce |
| 3½ oz/100 g | baby spinach |

This dish was named in honor of Le Rouet, the little village where Daniel Ettlinger lives. The combination of fish, wilted salad leaves, and baby spinach, is typical of the south of France.

For our recipe the chef has chosen salad leaves with a definite character and fine nuances of flavor, which perfectly complement tender baby spinach. This vegetable, which originated in Persia, has dark green, crinkly or smooth leaves, and contains numerous minerals and vitamins. During preparation, the leaves are washed well and sweated in olive oil until they wilt. You could use iceberg lettuce instead of the spinach. Depending on the time of year, Daniel Ettlinger also likes to use radicchio, whose bitter taste is reminiscent of curly endive. Arugula, the salad leaf from the area around Nice, has a peppery taste. If you use this salad leaf, there is no need to add pepper to the red mullet

fillets. You could also use nasturtium or dandelion leaves instead of the arugula.

When wilted, these leaves are all perfect with Mediterranean red mullet. If red mullet is difficult to obtain, red snapper can be used instead. If you have problems filleting fish, ask your fishmonger to do it for you.

To check when oil has reached the correct frying temperature, put the oil into a cold pan, with a little knob of butter in the middle. When the butter has melted the oil is at the correct temperature.

Desirée potatoes are available throughout the year. When the potato slices are baked in the oven, Daniel Ettlinger adds two slices of lemon, to create more flavor.

Scale the red mullet. Insert the knife behind the dorsal fin and work the knife down along the backbone, from head to tail, removing the fillets on either side. Remove the small bones from the fillets with a pair of tweezers.

Wash the potatoes, peel them, and cut them into slices about ¼ in/½ cm thick. Heat 1 tbsp olive oil in a sauté pan. Add the 4 unpeeled whole cloves of garlic. Fry the potatoes and garlic for about 3 minutes. Season to taste with salt and pepper.

Remove the potato slices from the pan and spread them with black olive paste, reserving a small quantity for use as a garnish. Wash and slice the tomatoes. Place a slice of tomato on top of each potato slice and put them back into the pan.

# "Le Rouet"

Fill the pan with fish or chicken stock until it comes halfway up the potatoes and tomatoes. Add two slices of lemon. Put the pan in the oven and bake for 20 minutes at 400 °F/200 °C.

Season the fish fillets with salt and pepper. Heat 1 tbsp olive oil in a skillet. Fry the fillets for 2 minutes, first on the skin side, then on the flesh side. Remove the fish from the pan and keep it warm.

Wilt the salad leaves in the skillet for 1 minute. Dress the leaves with a little cooking liquor from the potatoes, olive oil, half the chopped parsley, and black olive paste. Arrange the fish, wilted salad leaves, and baked potato slices on a plate. Sprinkle with the remaining parsley.

# Oyster Fritters

| | |
|---|---|
| Preparation time: | 30 minutes |
| Chilling time: | 1 hour |
| Cooking time: | 20 minutes |
| Difficulty: | ☆ |

**Serves 4**

| | |
|---|---|
| 2 dozen | Bouzigues or other large oysters |
| 8 oz/250 g | spinach |
| 1 tbsp | olive oil |
| 1 | shallot |
| ⅓ cup + 1½ tbsp/100 ml | Noilly Prat |

| | |
|---|---|
| 1 generous cup/250 ml | light cream |
| | salt, pepper |
| 4 cups/1 l | oil for frying |

**For the batter:**

| | |
|---|---|
| 2 scant cups/200 g | flour |
| 3 | eggs, separated |
| ½ cup/120 ml | beer |
| 1 cup/250 ml | milk |
| | salt |

**For the garnish:**

| | |
|---|---|
| | fresh chives |

Oysters in batter make an original appetizer. These shell-fish are usually eaten raw, or are enjoyed simply with lemon juice, or a vinegar and onion dressing.

Bouzigues oysters are specially farmed in southern France, more specifically in the Thau Basin. They take their name from a little village in Hérault which was known for its oysters even before the Roman invasion. Contrary to the widely prevailing opinion that oysters should only be eaten when there is an "r" in the month, the oyster farmers in the Thau Basin harvest the oysters all year round. Oysters are extremely sensitive. They must be stored in a dark, cool, well-ventilated place at a temperature between 41 and 59 degrees Fahrenheit (5 and 15 degrees Celsius). If you can't find large oysters, you could always use a smaller variety, such as Marennes, which contain less iodine.

After poaching, let the oysters rest in their shells, so that the juices are drawn out. They should be fried at the last minute.

When making the batter, ensure that you don't add too much egg white, otherwise the batter, when cooked, will not hold its shape.

The blanched spinach is wrapped around the oysters in order to protect them during cooking. It also imparts a delicate flavor to the batter. From time to time the chef uses sorrel too.

Because oysters contain iodine, the shallot dressing needs little salt. Noilly Prat is a sun-ripened vermouth with a very intensive flavor. It is typical of the area. You can substitute chardonnay, or even champagne.

*Put the oysters in a pan with just enough water to cover them. Bring to the boil and simmer for 8 minutes. Strain, reserving a little of the cooking liquor. Put the oysters into cold water to open, and discard any that do not open. Detach the meat from the shell, then put it back in the shell.*

*Batter: Beat together the flour, egg yolks, and salt. Beat in the beer and milk. In a separate bowl, beat the egg whites with a pinch of salt until stiff. Carefully fold the egg whites into the batter until a smooth, creamy mixture forms. Leave to rest for an hour in the refrigerator.*

*Pick over the spinach, removing the stalks. Bring a pan of salted water to the boil and blanch the spinach in it for 1 minute. Refresh the spinach in cold water, then wrap each oyster in a spinach leaf.*

# with Noilly Prat

Using a fork, dip the oysters in the batter until they are well coated.

Heat 1 tbsp olive oil in a skillet and sweat the chopped shallot for 3 minutes until softened. Add the Noilly Prat and simmer for 5 minutes. Add a little of the reserved oyster liquor and the cream, and simmer for 2 minutes. Season to taste. Blend, strain through a sieve, and keep warm.

Heat the oil in a deep pan until very hot. Fry the oysters for 2 minutes, then drain on kitchen paper. Place a spinach leaf in each oyster shell. Put an oyster fritter on top. Pour some of the sauce into a small bowl for dipping, garnish with chives, and serve with the oyster fritters.

# Bouzigues Oysters

Preparation time: 30 minutes
Cooking time: 20 minutes
Difficulty: ★★

**Serves 4**

16                Bouzigues or
                  other large oysters
8 oz/250 g        Swiss chard leaves
½ stick/60 g      butter
1 clove           garlic

3½ tbsp/50 g      poutargue (salted,
                    pressed and flattened
                    mullet roe; optional)
6½ tbsp/100 g     whipping cream
                  salt
                  freshly ground pepper
                  large quantity of
                    rock salt

Nowadays it is possible to enjoy oysters throughout the year. Thanks to advances in oyster farming, oysters are no longer limited to a certain time of year. The village of Bouzigues, in the Thau Basin, produces first-class oysters all year round.

Georges Rousset, Maître Cuisinier de France, prefers slightly bigger oysters. They are hollow and decidedly tasty, juicy, and plentiful. Large oysters are especially suitable for cooking. If you can't find Bouzigues oysters, you could use another kind of oyster or other shellfish, such as scallops. In each case the filling is made from Swiss chard.

To ensure that the oysters open, Monsieur Rousset recommends spreading the oysters on a baking sheet and baking them in an oven preheated to about 320 degrees Fahrenheit/160 degrees Celsius for ten minutes. Don't forget to reserve the juices that are drawn out.

We only use the green part of the Swiss chard in our recipe. You should remove the white ribs. Monsieur Rousset likes to add a hint of garlic to his recipe by spearing a peeled clove of garlic on the fork that is used to turn the Swiss chard during cooking.

This unusual appetizer also introduces another Mediterranean product, *poutargue*: salted, pressed, and flattened mullet roe, also sometimes known as *caviar de Martigues*. Don't add any salt when you use *poutargue*. By the way, this very special ingredient is not essential to this recipe – except for gourmets.

Open the oysters, remove the meat from the shells, and reserve. Collect the liquor, and strain it. Clean the oyster shells and wash the Swiss chard. Remove the white ribs, boil a pan of salted water and blanch the Swiss chard for 4 minutes. Drain the leaves, and chop them finely.

Melt a scant ⅛ stick/10 g butter in a skillet and add the chopped Swiss chard. Stir with a fork that has a peeled clove of garlic on the end. Add 1 tbsp cream and incorporate it into the chard. Fill the oyster shells with the Swiss chard, making a shallow well in the center.

Carefully place the oyster meat in a saucepan, add the reserved oyster liquor and a little salt and pepper, and poach them in their own juices for 4 minutes on each side, but don't let them boil. When they are almost cooked through, drain them, reserving the liquor.

# with Swiss Chard

Put a slice of poutargue (if using) in the middle of the Swiss chard. Place an oyster on top.

To make the sauce, bring the oyster cooking liquid to the boil and reduce it. Season with pepper. Add the rest of the cream and bring to the boil again, until a nice, smooth sauce forms. Beat in the rest of the butter.

Grate the remaining poutargue into the sauce. Warm it on low heat for 2 minutes, but do not let the sauce boil. Cover a deep dish in rock salt. Position each oyster shell securely in the salt so they can't tip over. Carefully spoon the hot sauce over the oysters, and serve immediately.

# Provençal

| Preparation time: | 1 hour |
| Fish soaking time: | 24 hours |
| Cooking time: | 1 hour |
| Difficulty: | ★ |

**Serves 4**

| 2¼ lb/1 kg | whelks |
| 4 | carrots |
| 8 | potatoes |
| 1 lb/500 g | green beans |
| ½ | cauliflower |
| 4 | globe artichokes |
| 4 | eggs |
| 2 | boiled beetroot |
| scant 1 lb/400 g | dried salt cod |

| 3 sprigs | fresh thyme |
| 1 | bay leaf |
| 10 | black peppercorns |

**Vegetables for the whelk stock:**

| 1 tbsp | black peppercorns |
| 1 | carrot |
| 1 | leek |
| 1 | onion |
| 1 | clove |
| 3 sprigs | fresh thyme |
| 1 | bay leaf |

**For the aioli dressing:**

| 8 cloves | garlic |
| 3 | egg yolks |
| 2 cups/500 ml | olive oil |
| 1 pinch | saffron |
| | salt, pepper |

It is often said in the Mediterranean that aioli is a true symbol of the south of France, because the vegetables eaten with it taste of sunshine. Our recipe is one for high days and holidays, when the whole family comes together; sometimes the whole village in the summer! It's really a main meal. If you want to serve it as such, you must of course increase the quantities for all the ingredients.

Aioli is a mayonnaise dressing, whose name is made up of the French for garlic, *ail*, and Provençal for oil, *oli*, both of which are ingredients in this recipe. Choose your garlic carefully; the bulb should be firm and, above all, dry. White garlic will keep for up to six months in a cool, dark place; purple garlic will keep for up to a year. You should also use a very good quality olive oil for this special recipe. Our chef only uses highly aromatic extra-virgin olive oil from the first, cold, pressing.

Use seasonal vegetables to ensure that they are fresh. The cauliflower should be very white; the best are available at the end of the summer. Choose a firm, waxy variety of potato, such as Charlotte, that keep their shape when boiled or steamed. Winkles are often served instead of whelks, or *petit gris* snails with their delicate flesh and rich flavor.

To remove the salt crust from the dried cod, scrub it well, then soak it for 24 hours. Change the water frequently. If you cut up the fish into chunks you'll speed up the salt removal. You could use fresh cod fillets instead.

Wash the whelks. Put them in a saucepan with just enough water to cover them. Add 1 tbsp black peppercorns and the rest of the stock vegetables: sliced carrot, thinly sliced leek (white only), sliced onion, clove, thyme, and bay leaf. Boil for 20 minutes.

Wash and peel the carrots, rinse the potatoes, top and tail the beans, and divide the cauliflower into florets. Trim the artichokes and remove the bottom leaves. Shorten the artichoke stalk by half and peel it. Boil a pan of water, add the eggs, and boil for 10 minutes, or until hard.

Boil all the vegetables separately in salt water. Cook the potatoes for 15 minutes, the carrots, artichokes, and cauliflower for 10 minutes, and the beans for 8 minutes. Plunge the cooked beetroot into a pan of boiling water to reheat them. Shell the eggs. Reserve all the vegetables.

# Banquet

Drain the salt cod. Bring a pan of water to the boil and add the salt cod, 3 sprigs thyme, bay leaf, and 10 peppercorns. Poach the fish for 5-6 minutes. Drain it and reserve.

To make the aioli, peel the garlic and remove the core. Crush in a mortar. Add salt, pepper, and 3 egg yolks.

Add the olive oil in a thin stream, beating the egg mixture all the time, until an emulsion forms. Add a pinch of saffron. Arrange the vegetables, fish, whelks strained from the stock, and hard boiled eggs on a large platter, and serve with the aioli.

Preparation time:    1 hour
Cooking time:    15 minutes
Difficulty:    ★★

**Serves 4**

**For the stuffed zucchini:**

| | |
|---|---|
| 6 | small zucchini |
| 4 | button mushrooms |
| 1 thick slice | boiled ham |
| 1 | medium onion |
| 2 tbsp | olive oil |

**For the stuffed tomatoes:**

| | |
|---|---|
| 4 | tomatoes, each 3 oz/80 g |
| 3 slices | white bread |
| 1 | onion |
| 1 clove | garlic |

| | |
|---|---|
| ¼ bunch | fresh parsley |
| 4 tbsp | olive oil |
| 3½ oz/100 g | ground beef or pork |
| 3 sprigs | fresh thyme |

**For the stuffed mushrooms:**

| | |
|---|---|
| 4 | mushrooms, each 2 oz/50 g |
| 1 | onion |
| 1 clove | garlic |
| 1 oz/30 g | bacon |
| 2 tbsp | olive oil |

**For the stuffed onions:**

| | |
|---|---|
| 4 | onions, each 3½ oz/100 g |
| ¼ stick/30 g | butter |
| 1 | egg yolk |
| 8 tsp/40 g | grated Gruyère |
| 4 tbsp | whipping cream |
| | |
| 2 cups/500 ml | vegetable stock |
| 2 tbsp | olive oil |
| | salt, pepper |

Stuffed baby vegetables are a typical southern French dish. Francis Robin is especially fond of them and has refined the recipe by filling each vegetable he uses with a different stuffing.

Because the quality of the vegetables should be perfect, this recipe requires a certain degree of patience to prepare. There is lots of preparation to do before stuffing each of the vegetables.

Here are a few tips to help you succeed. Use a melon baller to help you hollow out the vegetables. You could use a teaspoon too. It is important that you don't pierce the vegetable's skin.

You could use tenderer and milder flavored baby onions, available from April to the end of June. Note that they take a little longer to cook. Insert a sharp knife into the onion to check whether it is done.

Choose mushrooms with big heads that are easy to stuff. You should brown the chopped mushrooms and stalks quickly, otherwise they discolor. When choosing zucchini, make sure they are small, straight, and firm. They taste much better than big ones.

Choose a firm variety of tomato that will keep its shape well when cooked. Depending on what's available in your area, you could also stuff other vegetables, such as eggplant, leeks, or potatoes.

*Wash the zucchini and pat dry. Cut into 1½ in/4 cm-long chunks, and hollow out, reserving the flesh. Blanch the zucchini for 5–6 minutes. Drain and put aside. Chop the reserved zucchini flesh, button mushrooms, and ham. Peel and chop the onion. Put aside all filling ingredients.*

*Heat 2 tbsp olive oil in a skillet and add the reserved filling ingredients to the pan. Sauté them for 2 minutes. Slice the tops off the tomatoes, and carefully scoop out the flesh. Cut the white bread into ¼–½ in/1 cm dice. Peel and chop the onion and garlic. Chop the parsley.*

*Heat 2 tbsp olive oil in a skillet, add the onion, parsley, and garlic and sauté with the ground beef or pork, chopped thyme, salt and pepper for 15 minutes. Heat 2 tbsp olive oil in another skillet, and sauté 5 tbsp diced bread. Add 3 tbsp croutons to the tomato filling, and put it aside.*

# Vegetables

Remove the mushroom stalks and clean the undersides of the cups. Chop the stalks, peel and chop the onion and garlic. Dice the bacon. Heat 2 tbsp olive oil and sauté the mushroom stalks, onion, garlic and bacon. Add the remaining croutons and season to taste.

Peel the onions and boil in salted water for 20 minutes. Slice the tops off the onions and scoop out. Heat the butter in a skillet. Chop the onion flesh and sweat it in the butter until translucent. Remove from the pan and combine with the egg yolk, cheese, and cream. Season to taste.

Sprinkle salt inside the vegetables. Fill each vegetable. Place them in a deep baking sheet filled with the stock and 2 tbsp olive oil. Bake in the oven pre-heated to 400 °F/200 °C for 25 minutes. Take out of the oven, drizzle over the remaining olive oil, and serve hot.

# Artichoke Millefeuilles

| Preparation time: | 25 minutes |
| Marinating time: | 1 hour |
| Cooking time: | 10 minutes |
| Difficulty: | ★ |

**Serves 4**

| 5 oz/150 g | young goat milk cheese |
| 8 | globe artichokes |
| 3 tbsp | olive oil |
| few sprigs | fresh thyme |
| 2 cloves | garlic |
| generous ¾ cup/ 200 ml | oil for frying |
| 3½ oz/100 g | arugula |
| | salt, pepper |

**For the marinade:**

| 2 tbsp | balsamic vinegar |
| 3 tbsp | olive oil |

| | salt |
| | pepper |

**For the balsamic vinaigrette:**

| ½ tsp | salt |
| 1 tbsp | balsamic vinegar |
| 1 tbsp | wine vinegar |
| 1 tbsp | candied root ginger syrup |
| 4 tbsp | olive oil |
| ½ tsp | salt, pinch of pepper |

**For the garnish:**

| 1 | sun-dried tomato |
| 3 | celery sticks, with leaves |
| | parmesan |
| | rock salt |

This appetizer, with young goat milk cheese, is a down-to-earth dish. Our chef prepares it with Gorbio, a goat milk cheese made in the Nice area. You could also use Crottin de Chavignol. Let the cheese marinate for as long as possible, so it takes on the slightly sweet taste of the balsamic vinegar.

If you can find them, buy spiny globe artichokes, with a slightly bitterer taste. These artichokes come from Sicily and are members of the thistle family. The globe sits on the base of the flower and is surrounded by leaves. When the choke is removed, the meaty, soft artichoke heart makes good eating. The fleshy lower part of the leaves is also delicious. The artichoke, introduced to France by Catherine de Médicis, has long been used as a medicine. They will keep for a couple of days if the stalk is put in water, like a flower. Artichoke hearts should be put into water acidulated with lemon immediately, otherwise they discolor. If your artichoke hearts are too big, you can cut them in half.

Garlic tastes sweeter if it is blanched. Peel it and immerse it alternately in cold and boiling water; repeat the process three times. If desired, you can season the sautéed slices of artichoke with celery salt. You can use curly endive instead of arugula.

When preparing the millefeuilles, layer the goat milk cheese and sautéed artichokes on top of each other. Finish off with the fried garlic and one or two parmesan shavings. Then add the celery leaves, the sun-dried tomato, and a couple of grains of rock salt. Prepare the millefeuille in advance if you like more intense flavors, but the salad should only be dressed at the last moment.

*Cut the goat milk cheese into slices that are ½–¾ in/1–2 cm thick. Allow 3 slices per millefeuille. Beat together the ingredients for the marinade, pour them over the cheese, and marinate for 1 hour.*

*Cut off the artichoke stalks and remove the leaves down to the base. Scoop out the choke with a spoon. Cut the artichoke hearts into slices that are about ¼ in/2–3 mm thick.*

*Heat 3 tbsp olive oil in a skillet and sauté the artichoke slices. Season to taste with salt, pepper, and some rubbed thyme. Drain the slices on kitchen paper.*

# with Goat Milk Cheese

Peel the garlic and cut into slivers. Blanch the garlic, then drain it. Heat the oil in a pan and fry the garlic, keeping the slivers moving so they don't stick together.

To make the vinaigrette, beat together the salt and balsamic vinegar. Add the wine vinegar, ginger syrup, olive oil, and pepper. Beat again, adding 1 tbsp water.

Build up the millefeuille in 3 layers, alternating a slice of goat milk cheese and a slice of artichoke. Finish off with fried garlic and parmesan shavings. Toss the salad in the vinaigrette, arrange on a plate with the millefeuille, and garnish.

# Green Cabbage Rösti

Preparation time: 20 minutes
Cooking time: 50 minutes
Difficulty: ★

**Serves 4**

| | |
|---|---|
| 12 | thin slices bacon |
| 5 oz/150 g | slab of bacon |
| ½ head | green cabbage |
| 1 | thin salami |
| 2 tbsp | drippings |
| 1 loaf | rye bread |

rock salt
salt
pepper

**For the garnish:**
| | |
|---|---|
| 1 | scallion (optional) |
| 4 | cherry tomatoes |

This appetizer is a traditional dish from Cerdagne, a region in the Pyrénées-Orientales department of France, which was partitioned by France and Spain in 1659. The farmers originally prepared this meal with Savoy cabbage, a variety of green cabbage traditionally harvested after the first frosts. They cooked it with drippings and pork belly. Jean-Claude Vila has taken this rustic recipe and brought it right up to date.

Pork belly is no longer cooked with the cabbage. Instead it appears in the form of thin, crispy, fried rolls of bacon that are a wonderful complement to the soft cabbage. Sometimes, poverty dictated that the farmers had to use spoilt, blemished cabbages, but you should ensure that your cabbage is firm, with tightly closed leaves without holes.

Before preparing the dish, remove the outer layer of cabbage leaves. Blanch the green cabbage in boiling, salted water for five minutes. Carry out this process three times, changing the water each time. Then let the cabbage drain, and finally refresh it in ice water. According to our chef, sautéing the cabbage is important. It should be nicely browned and all the steam should have evaporated.

Drippings are made from the fat that runs from fried bacon (or pork belly). It is mostly used for long cooking times because of its creamy consistency.

The usual accompaniment to this dish is a slice of rye bread. Rye comes from Anatolia and the area around Turkistan, growing in the mountainous areas on poor soils. Rye flour produces dark, heavy bread. It has a slightly acidic taste and keeps well.

*Lay 8 slices of bacon side by side on a baking sheet and cover them with another baking sheet. Preheat the oven to 350 °F/180 °C and bake the bacon for about 15 minutes. Roll up the remaining slices and put them aside for the garnish.*

*Finely dice the slab of bacon. Dry-fry it in a large skillet, until crisp and brown.*

*Bring a pan of salted water to the boil. Blanch the cabbage in it for 5 minutes. Change the water and repeat the process twice more. Drain the cabbage, refresh in ice water, and dice.*

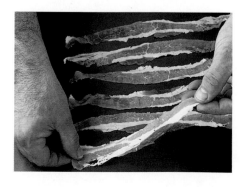

# with Bacon Sails

Cut off a few slices of salami for the garnish. Of the remaining salami, dice one half, and very finely chop the other. Add the salami to the pan with the bacon and sauté it for 5 minutes.

Add the cabbage and the drippings to the skillet. Press the mixture down firmly, and sauté it for 10 minutes.

Cut out rounds of cabbage mixture. Transfer to the center of a plate. Arrange the slices of salami and bacon rolls around the cabbage. Arrange a slice of the crisp bacon on top of each cabbage round, like a sail. Add scallion rings and a cherry tomato. Serve with rye bread.

# Onion, Olive, and Anchovy

Preparation time:   20 minutes
Cooking time:       40 minutes
Difficulty:         ★

**Serves 4**
**For the onion, olive, and anchovy bruschetta:**

| | |
|---|---|
| 4 | white onions |
| 2 cloves | garlic |
| 3 tbsp | olive oil |
| 1 sprig | fresh thyme |
| 9 | anchovy fillets in oil |
| 1 slice | bacon |
| 4 slices | whole-wheat bread |
| 10 oz/300 g | seasonal salad |
| 2 oz/50 g | baby spinach |

| | |
|---|---|
| ½ cup/100 g | black olives, pitted |
| 2 tbsp | white wine vinegar |
| 4 | eggs |
| | salt |
| | pepper |

**For the balsamic vinaigrette:**

| | |
|---|---|
| 1 tbsp | balsamic vinegar |
| 3 tbsp | olive oil |
| | salt |
| | pepper |

**For the garnish:**

| | |
|---|---|
| 4 | black olives |
| 1 | scallion (green) |

In Nice, this onion, olive, and anchovy tart, known as *pissaladière*, is the favorite snack. Originally this savory pastry was known as *pissalat*, and was made with anchovies preserved in brine. They could be stored in stoneware jars throughout the year and added to any sauce or dressing.

In time, toasted bread was added, and a garnish of anchovies, onions, and black olives. Today, *pissaladière* is one of the most important elements in Nice's culinary legacy. Our chef serves this dish with a poached egg and baby salad leaves.

Anchovies are little saltwater fish. They are a maximum of 8 inches/20 centimeters long, greenish-yellow on the back, and have a shimmering, silvery belly. They are plentiful in the Mediterranean Sea. The fish can be bought fresh and whole, or filleted and preserved in salt. Fillets preserved

in oil are also available, in cans. At any rate, be careful when seasoning this dish, because the anchovy fillets that you need are already salted. When choosing onions, our chef suggests white or red, because they are very juicy and soften easily.

When preparing this appetizer, it's important to poach the egg at the last minute. Because the water has been acidulated with vinegar, the egg white will form a pocket around the yolk. You should not salt the water. Our chef suggests that after poaching the egg, you rinse it briefly under running water to remove the vinegary taste.

Depending on the time of year, Daniel Ettlinger accompanies his *pissaladière* with 2 ounces/50 grams arugula, 2 ounces/50 grams corn salad, and a little curly endive. These salad varieties are refreshing and their delicate flavor is heightened by the balsamic vinaigrette.

Peel the onions, cut them into quarters, and slice them. Peel the garlic cloves, cut them into quarters, and slice them.

Heat 1 tbsp olive oil in a saucepan. Add the onions, garlic, and thyme, and sweat them until translucent. Add the anchovy fillets and slice of bacon. Season the onion mixture sparingly with salt and pepper. Cover and sweat for about 30 minutes on low heat.

Preheat the oven to 400 °F/200 °C. Drizzle olive oil over the slices of bread and bake them in the oven for approximately 3 minutes. Wash the salad leaves along with the spinach.

# Bruschetta with Poached Egg

Take the sprig of thyme and slice of bacon out of the pan. Spread the onion mixture onto the toasted bread.

Arrange the anchovy fillets and a few pitted olives on top of the onion mixture. Bring a saucepan of water to the boil and add the vinegar. One by one break the eggs into a cup, slide them into the boiling water, and poach them for 4 minutes.

For the vinaigrette, combine the salt and pepper, beat in the balsamic vinegar, then the olive oil. Toss the salad leaves in the dressing. Drain the poached eggs. On each plate arrange a slice of onion bread, salad leaves, and a poached egg. Garnish with chopped olives and green scallion.

# Fried Garbanzo

Preparation time: 35 minutes
Cooking time: 25 minutes
Difficulty: ★

**Serves 4**

⅓ cup + 1½ tbsp/100 ml   olive oil
1 scant cup/150 g   garbanzo flour
   oil for frying
   salt

**For the tomato sauce:**

| | |
|---|---|
| 5 | tomatoes |
| 1 | small onion |
| 1 | shallot |
| 1 tbsp | olive oil |
| 10 | black olives |
| 1 pinch | cayenne pepper |
| 2 | anchovy fillets in oil |

**For the bouquet garni:**

| | |
|---|---|
| 2 | bay leaves |
| 1 sprig | fresh thyme |
| 2 sprigs | fresh flat-leaf parsley |

In the Marseilles of the 1930s, the mobile traders in the Old Harbor loudly proclaimed the popularity of their *panisses*, garbanzo flour pancakes, which were a local specialty at the time. Now they are available the length of the Mediterranean coast. In the south of France they are sometimes called "poor man's bread."

Without doubt, this dish is one of the cornerstones of Mediterranean cuisine. The garbanzo bean is a pulse, which for centuries has formed part of dishes such as couscous, braised beef, stews, ragouts, or *olla podrida*, the Spanish version of French *pot-au-feu*, or one-pot stew. It appears in the form of small balls in the Near East, which are known as *falafel*. *Hummus*, garbanzo bean purée, originated there too.

Garbanzo beans have been known throughout Europe since the Middle Ages. They are available dried, or canned. The dried beans are soaked in cold water overnight, with a little baking soda, to soften them, so they are easier to digest.

When using garbanzo flour, make sure it cooks slowly and doesn't form lumps. Georges Rousset says that in the past, garbanzo beans were always cooked with a bay leaf. Our chef recommends that you use aromatic, clear, cold-pressed olive oil.

You could also serve your garbanzo bean dumplings with a side salad. If you have a couple of dumplings left over, simply serve them with a different sauce a couple of days later. They can be served sprinkled with grated parmesan and baked, covered with sliced mushroom, or coated in pesto, a sauce made from basil, garlic, toasted pine nuts, and olive oil.

*Pour 2 cups of water into a saucepan with the olive oil, and a pinch of salt, and bring it to the boil.*

*Take the pan off the heat. Gradually stir the garbanzo flour into the saucepan, stirring carefully to prevent lumps from forming.*

*Put the pan back on the burner on low heat, and simmer for 15 minutes. Stir constantly to help the mixture thicken, and prevent it burning.*

# Bean Dumplings

When the mixture has formed a thick paste, use it to fill individual patty tins. Leave them to cool. Tomato sauce: Pour boiling water over the tomatoes in a bowl. Leave for a few minutes, drain, skin and deseed them, then chop the flesh. Peel and finely chop the onion and shallot.

Fry the chopped onion and shallot, add the tomatoes, and bouquet garni. When the sauce has combined and reduced, remove the bouquet garni. Purée the sauce and heat it in the pan. Add the chopped olives, cayenne, and anchovies, and simmer for 2 minutes.

Take the garbanzo flour dumplings out of the patty tins. Heat the oil for frying until very hot, and fry the dumplings for 2 minutes, until golden brown. Serve the dumplings hot on a bed of the tomato sauce with olives and anchovies.

# Marseilles

Preparation time: 15 minutes
Cooking time: 15 minutes
Difficulty: ★

**Serves 4**

| | |
|---|---|
| 1½–2 lb/ | |
| 800 g | filleted fish (sea bass, red gurnard, John Dory, ocean perch, scallops, shelled shrimp, rock lobster) |
| 1 | red bell pepper |
| 1 | green bell pepper |
| 4 | tomatoes |
| 3 | shallots |
| 1 bunch | fresh chives |

**For the vinaigrette:**

| | |
|---|---|
| 2 | lemons |
| generous ¾ cup/ | |
| 200 ml | olive oil |
| | salt |
| | pepper |
| | Tabasco sauce |

**For the fish stock:**

| | |
|---|---|
| 3 sprigs | fresh thyme |
| 1 | star anise |
| 3 strips | dried fennel |
| 10 | black peppercorns |
| 10 | white peppercorns |
| | salt |

This appetizer by Jean-Michel Minguella is a splendid way to showcase many types of fish; he has hooked just about every delicious Mediterranean variety.

Whether you use sea bass, monkfish, red gurnard, or ocean perch, take care that they are absolutely fresh, have bright scales, and don't smell unpleasant. The gills must be a nice, bright red. The shellfish must also be very fresh.

It's easiest if you ask your fishmonger to fillet the fish for you, then all you will have to do is remove the last few bones with a pair of tweezers. If you can't find any of the above fish, you could use grouper, tuna or bonito, swordfish, or leer fish.

If you're feeling generous, substitute langoustines for the rock lobster – much more elegant! For this recipe you need white fish that stays firm when cooked in the stock.

If using shellfish, cook separately in boiling water for 10 minutes, so that no grit from the shells comes into contact with the fish.

Buy the freshest bell peppers, with firm, green stalks, and no blemishes or wrinkles.

This is a healthy dish, because little fat is needed to prepare it, and it relies on high-quality olive oil. This golden-green liquid is a tasty addition to this Mediterranean delicacy. Ensure that it is extra-virgin olive oil.

*Fillet the fish. Open the scallops and remove the meat. Cut the shrimp and the rock lobster in half lengthwise.*

*Cut the red and green bell peppers into thin strips. Put the tomatoes in a bowl and pour boiling water over them. Leave them for a few minutes, then drain, skin, deseed, and dice them. Peel and chop the shallots. Chop a few chive stalks.*

*To make the stock, bring 6 cups/1.5 l water to the boil with the thyme, star anise, dried fennel, black and white peppercorns, and salt.*

# Fish Salad

To make the vinaigrette, juice the lemons. Beat the juice together with the olive oil and 3½ tbsp/50 ml lukewarm water. Season to taste with salt, pepper, and a dash of Tabasco sauce.

Poach the fish fillets and the cooked shellfish (if using; see above) in the stock for 5 minutes. Drain them and put aside.

Mix the chives, shallots, bell peppers, and tomatoes with the fish fillets. Arrange them decoratively on a plate. Pour the vinaigrette over the fish, and garnish with a couple of stalks of chive.

# Soups

# Catalan

Preparation time: 10 minutes
Cooking time: 20 minutes
Difficulty: ★

**Serves 4**

| | |
|---|---|
| 1 bulb | garlic |
| 1 sprig | thyme |
| 2 slices | stale white bread, diced |
| 2 | egg yolks |
| 2 tbsp | olive oil |

rock salt
salt
pepper

**For the garnish:**
fresh chives

This traditional Catalan soup is quick and easy to prepare. The recipe is very popular in Spain. During the cold season it is worth enjoying this dish regularly, as it helps build up the immune system, and is invigorating.

Since the dawn of time, mankind has ascribed every possible virtue to garlic. Garlic is encountered as a vegetable, as a seasoning, or flavoring, in every Mediterranean recipe. It originated from the steppes of Central Asia. In Catalan it is called *all*, as it is in Celtic, in which language the word means "burning." Hippocrates described garlic as "hot, slightly laxative, and healthy." As a result of the Crusades it spread throughout Europe, where it was regarded as a miracle cure – it can be used to ward off the Plague and, occasionally, vampires. Garlic is harvested in July and August. Garlic from the south of France is regarded as the very best. It flourishes in Provence and the department of Midi-Pyrénées. There are different varieties: white, purple, and pink, but they all have the same intense flavor. For this recipe Jean Plouzennec blanches the garlic several times to prevent the flavor being too strong.

When you buy garlic, the bulbs should be very firm and dry. Did you know that each bulb has 12–16 cloves? Fresh garlic is best kept in your refrigerator's salad compartment. The garlic you need in order to keep away the Plague and vampires is best stored in the driest place in your kitchen.

Garlic does not tolerate storage in damp conditions. It will quickly germinate or grow mold. When you have peeled and chopped a clove, you should use it as soon as possible, because it oxidizes quickly and the taste suffers. Remove the green or white core to ensure that the garlic will be easy to digest.

*Peel the garlic. Remove the cores from the center of each clove, using a sharp knife if necessary. Put the cloves of garlic in a pan with enough water to cover.*

*Bring the pan of water with the garlic to the boil. Drain off the water, refill the pan, and bring the water to the boil again, to blanch the garlic. Season the garlic with salt, and drain the cloves.*

*Bring 4 cups/1 l slightly salted water to the boil, add the garlic and sprig of thyme, and simmer for 10–15 minutes. Take the thyme out after 5–7 minutes, so its flavor does not overpower that of the garlic.*

# Garlic Soup

At the end of the cooking time, purée the garlic with a hand-held blender. Bring the soup to the boil again over low heat, and season it to taste with salt and pepper.

Add the diced bread. Wait until it is completely soft, then purée it into the soup with the blender.

Beat in the egg yolks and the olive oil. Garnish the soup with chives and serve it immediately.

# Cream of Pumpkin

Preparation time: 20 minutes
Cooking time: 40 minutes
Difficulty: ★

**Serves 4**

| | |
|---|---|
| 1 | onion |
| 1 tbsp | olive oil |
| 1½ cups/250 g | pumpkin |
| 1 clove | garlic |
| 1 cup/250 ml | chicken stock |

| | |
|---|---|
| 1 cup/250 ml | light cream |
| | salt |
| | pepper |
| 1 pinch | grated nutmeg |
| | juice of ½ lemon |
| 1 bunch | fresh chives |

**For the garnish:**

| | |
|---|---|
| 1 tbsp | olive oil |

This cream of pumpkin soup with chives is a wonderful way to get children to eat soup. It's easy to prepare, and its sweetness and color are reminiscent of the beautiful Provençal countryside.

The term "pumpkin" covers a wide variety of fruits, such as the calabash, marrow (giant zucchini), and Hokkaido pumpkin. These members of the pumpkin family originate from Asia, Africa, and America. They are round, voluminous, and colored red and yellow, inside and out. They appear on plates in the winter in the form of soup, baked *au gratin*, mashed, or baked as a sweet pie. Provençal pumpkin is brownish and slightly sweet, like the calabash. Our chef cooks pumpkin in chicken stock.

The chef sweats the onions, so that the soup develops a full flavor, but they should not brown. Onions originally came from Asia and have been cultivated for over 5,000 years. They consist of fleshy, white leaves surrounded by a papery yellow, brown, red, or white skin. Christian Étienne prefers using brown onions.

Ground nutmeg is indispensable in this recipe, because it heightens the pumpkin's flavor. This spice, originating from Southeast Asia, has a very spicy and intense aroma.

Chive, a relative of onions and garlic, has an onion-like taste. It is used fresh, chopped into little rings.

The success of this dish depends on the ingredients. If any of them is omitted, the cream of pumpkin soup will lose its delicious aroma.

Peel and slice the onion. Heat 1 tbsp olive oil in a pan and sweat the onion in it.

Peel the pumpkin, removing the seeds and fibers. Cut the pumpkin flesh into small dice. Crush the garlic. Add the diced pumpkin and crushed garlic to the onion, and mix well.

Pour the chicken stock into the pan, and simmer for 15 minutes, stirring frequently, until the liquid has evaporated.

# Soup with Chives

Stir in the cream and simmer the soup for a further 15 minutes. Season to taste with salt and pepper.

Pass the cream of pumpkin soup through a sieve, so the texture is nice and smooth. Add a pinch of ground nutmeg.

To heighten the pumpkin taste, fold in the lemon juice and chopped chives. Serve in soup cups or deep bowls, garnished with a drizzle of olive oil.

# Bouillabaisse

Preparation time: 20 minutes
Cooking time: 1 hour
Difficulty: ★

**Serves 8–10**

| | |
|---|---|
| 2 | onions |
| 4 cloves | garlic |
| 3 tbsp | olive oil |
| 3 | tomatoes |
| 1 tbsp | tomato paste |
| 1 piece | dried fennel |
| | weighing 3½ oz/100 g |
| 3 envelopes | saffron |
| 2¼ lb/1 kg | rock fish |
| 4 | large potatoes |

| | |
|---|---|
| 2 | scorpion fish, |
| | each 14 oz/400 g |
| 3 | gurnard, each 7 oz/200 g |
| 1 lb 10 oz/800 g | monkfish |

| | |
|---|---|
| 1 lb 10 oz/800g | conger eel |
| 3 | weever fish, |
| | each 7 oz/200 g |
| 2¼ lb/1 kg | John Dory |
| 4 | rock lobster |
| | salt, pepper |

**For the garlic mayonnaise (rouille):**

| | |
|---|---|
| 3 | egg yolks |
| 8 cloves | garlic |
| 2 cups/500 ml | olive oil |
| | salt, powdered saffron |

**For the croutons:**

| | |
|---|---|
| 1 | thin baguette |
| 5 cloves | garlic |
| 2 tbsp | olive oil |

Bouillabaisse, a very special fish soup from Marseilles, is famous throughout the world. The word *bouillabaisse* comes from the Provençal *bouïa-baisso*, roughly meaning "cooked on a low flame." In the past, the soup was first boiled up, before continuing to simmer on a low flame.

This soup was a simple fisherman's meal. Sea water was used for cooking, with the fish simmering in the water just as they had been caught. Nowadays bouillabaisse has become a classic dish and is a particular specialty of the "Miramar," our chef's restaurant.

In 1980 this fish soup became the subject of a legal directive, specifying which fish can be used in this recipe: gurnard, weever fish, John Dory, monkfish, conger eel, scorpion fish, and rock lobster. You can choose whatever is available. Jean-Michel Minguella advises using six varieties of fish, but you can use just four.

Whilst the fish are cooking you should keep your eye on them and take them out of the pan as soon as they are cooked. To enjoy the splendor of this dish, bring the fish to the table whole, and portion it there.

Make the essential hot, red, garlic mayonnaise (*rouille*) in the blender like ordinary mayonnaise. Season the egg yolk with salt, and add finely chopped garlic. To rescue mayonnaise which has separated, add an ice cube to the blender while it is running, and as if by magic, the ingredients will form a smooth, creamy emulsion.

*Peel and finely chop the onions and garlic. Heat 3 tbsp olive oil in a large pan, add the onions and garlic, and fry until softened. Cut the tomatoes into quarters and add them with the tomato paste, dried fennel, and 2 envelopes of saffron to the pan.*

*Add the rock fish and enough water to cover. Season with salt, and simmer for 20 minutes. Strain the fish and vegetables, reserving the broth. Purée the fish and vegetables. Strain the soup and return it to the pan. Simmer for a further 10 minutes and put aside.*

*Peel the potatoes and slice them lengthwise into ¾ in/2 cm-thick slices. Pour some of the reserved fish broth into a long fish kettle and add the potatoes.*

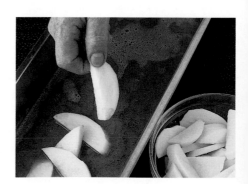

# "Miramar"

Place the scorpion fish, gurnard, monk-fish, conger eel, weever fish, John Dory, and rock lobster in the fish kettle, starting with the biggest, and finishing with the smallest.

Pour the remaining broth over the fish and season. Add the rest of the saffron. Cook at a rolling boil for 5 minutes, then simmer for 30 minutes on low heat. To make the mayonnaise, beat the egg yolks, add the salt, garlic, and saffron, then beat in the olive oil, drop by drop.

Slice the baguette into ¼ in/1 cm-thick slices. Rub them with garlic and drizzle olive oil over them. Bake the slices on a baking sheet in the oven at a temperature of 400 °F/200 °C. Spread rouille on 4 of them. Float one on each serving of soup. Strain the fish and serve with the soup.

# "Nice" Minestrone

| Preparation time: | 2 hours |
|---|---|
| Soaking time: | 8 hours |
| Cooking time: | 40 minutes |
| Difficulty: | ★★ |

**Serves 4**

| | |
|---|---|
| 8 cups/2 l | chicken stock |
| 3½ oz/100 g | baby squid |
| 3½ oz/100 g | macaroni |
| 1 or 2 | scallions |
| 4 tsp/20 g | chives |
| | salt, pepper |

**For the soup vegetables:**

| | |
|---|---|
| 3½ oz/100 g | pearl onions |
| 2 oz/50 g | shallots |
| 3½ oz/100 g | fennel |

| | |
|---|---|
| 3½ oz/100 g | carrots |
| 3½ oz/100 g | kohlrabi |
| 3½ oz/100 g | navy beans |
| 3½ oz/100 g | cauliflower |
| 3½ oz/100 g | waxy potatoes |

| | |
|---|---|
| 3½ oz/100g | fresh peas |
| 3½ oz/100 g | green beans |
| 3½ oz/100 g | zucchini |
| 3½ tbsp/40 g | sun-dried tomatoes |
| 1 tbsp | olive oil |

**For the basil sauce (pistou):**

| | |
|---|---|
| 3 cloves | garlic, peeled |
| 6 | basil leaves |
| 3 | sun-dried tomatoes |
| 4 tsp/20 g | pine nuts |
| 4 tbsp | olive oil |
| | salt, pepper |

**For the bouquet garni:**

| | |
|---|---|
| | thyme |
| | bay leaf |
| | parsley |

Minestrone, an Italian vegetable soup, always contains pasta, sometimes rice. Most important are the types of vegetables, which vary from region to region. In Tuscany navy beans are essential. Minestrone is often served with bread rubbed with garlic and olive oil. Elsewhere, the soup is served sprinkled with grated cheese.

You need fresh vegetables for our recipe. The navy beans should not soak for more than eight hours, otherwise harmful byproducts will form. Add the bouquet garni whilst the beans are cooking, but do not add salt, or they won't soften.

Macaroni, which is part of minestrone, is supposed to have originated in Arabia. It can be replaced by tagliatelle, which must be cut into pieces. It was our chef's idea to liven up this vegetable soup by adding baby squid. Clean the squid thoroughly, removing the head (reserving the tentacles), quill, and skin, before rinsing under running water. To ensure that the squid stay tender, put a couple of wine corks in the water so that the water stays below boiling point.

*Pistou*, which is only added at the end, is a Provençal seasoning, made from fresh, chopped basil, pine nuts, garlic, and sometimes sun-dried tomatoes. The ingredients are crushed in a mortar and beaten together with olive oil.

Parmesan cheese and rice should be omitted from this soup. Depending on the time of year you could add a couple of boletus mushrooms (ceps or porcini).

*Wash and prepare the soup vegetables. Dice them finely. Dice the sun-dried tomatoes and shuck the peas.*

*Heat 1 tbsp olive oil in a deep skillet. Sweat the onions, shallots, fennel, and carrots for 3–4 minutes, but don't let them go brown.*

*Add the chicken stock. Then add the bouquet garni, plus the kohlrabi, navy beans, cauliflower, and potatoes. Simmer for 15 minutes, then add the peas, green beans, zucchini, and tomatoes, and simmer for another 10 minutes.*

# with Squid

Prepare the squid as described above. Wash the squid well, and plunge them into boiling water to blanch, then add a couple of wine corks to prevent the water boiling any more. Blanch the squid for 2 minutes, then drain.

Bring a pan of salted water to the boil, add the macaroni and cook until it is "al dente." Drain the macaroni and cut into ¼ in/½ cm rings. In a blender, purée together all the ingredients for the pistou.

Add the squid to the vegetable soup, with the macaroni, chopped scallions, and chopped chives. Remove the bouquet garni. Finally stir in the pistou. Season to taste with salt and pepper, and serve hot.

# Mussels in Cream of

| Preparation time: | 30 minutes |
| Cooking time: | 40 minutes |
| Difficulty: | ★ |

**Serves 4**

| | |
| --- | --- |
| 4½ lb/2 kg | mussels |
| 1 cup/250 ml | dry white wine |
| 6 tbsp | olive oil |
| 2 slices | white bread |
| 3 cloves | garlic |
| 1 | carrot |
| 1 | leek |
| 1 | onion |
| 1 lb/500 g | assorted rock fish |
| 1½ tsp | saffron strands |
| | salt |
| | pepper |
| 2 cups/500 g | heavy cream |

**For the garnish:**

| | |
| --- | --- |
| | fresh chives |
| | ground saffron |

The Bouzigues mussels in the cream of rock fish soup get their name from a little village in the Languedoc region. Mussels are typically grown on lines in the Mediterranean area. Back in Roman times, mussels and oysters were harvested from natural mussel beds.

Sort the mussels carefully. They must be tightly closed and should not look dried out. Use them within three days of purchase. You should discard mussels with cracked or half-open shells. Before cooking them, the mussels are cleaned by removing their beards. To do this you need to scrub the shells under running water.

For this soup, Angel Yagues maintains that it's worth switching off the burner a couple of minutes before the specified time. The mussels then finish cooking, cool down, and you can remove them from their shells sooner.

Gurnard, weever fish, and scorpion fish are examples of rock fish. Don't forget smaller varieties. If you have problems obtaining these fish, ask your fishmonger for sole trimmings, which will also lend flavor to your soup.

This mussel soup goes wonderfully well with saffron. Whether in the shape of brownish strands, or yellowish-red powder, this famous spice comes from the stamens of a bulbed plant of the crocus family. It is characterized by its piquant smell and bitter taste.

You could substitute chervil or parsley for the chives.

*Rinse and clean the mussels. Put them in a pan with the white wine, bring to the boil, cover, and simmer for about 5 minutes. Strain the mussels, reserving the broth.*

*Take the meat out of the mussels and set it aside to cool. Heat 3 tbsp olive oil in a skillet. Fry the white bread in the oil, and take it out of the skillet. Let it cool, then rub it with one of the peeled garlic cloves. Cut out 4 rounds using a round cookie cutter.*

*Wash, peel, and dice the carrot, leek and onion. Chop the garlic cloves.*

# Rock Fish Soup

Heat 3 tbsp olive oil in a pan. Add the vegetables and sweat them in the oil for 5 minutes. Add the cleaned and gutted rock fish.

To make the fish soup, strain the mussel broth through a very fine sieve to filter out the dirt. Pour the broth over the fish and vegetables, and add the saffron strands. Season to taste with salt and pepper. Cook the soup on low heat for 20 minutes.

Pass the soup through a chinoise, or sieve, and return it to the pan. Bring it to the boil, simmer for 5 minutes, then stir in the cream. Season to taste. Arrange a circle of mussels in a dish. Pour in the soup. Put a slice of fried bread in the center. Garnish with saffron and chopped chives.

# Shrimp Soup

Preparation time: 40 minutes
Cooking time: 20 minutes
Difficulty: ✮

**Serves 4**

| | |
|---|---|
| 1 bunch | scallions |
| 4 cloves | garlic |
| 1 | white onion |
| 3 tbsp | olive oil |
| scant ⅛ stick/10 g | butter |
| generous ¼ cup/50 g | medium yellow cornmeal (polenta) |

| | |
|---|---|
| 2 cups/500 ml | chicken stock |
| 12 | large shrimp |
| 1 pinch | hot ground paprika |
| | salt |

**For the garnish:**

| | |
|---|---|
| 1 | white onion |
| scant ⅛ cup/10 g | flour |
| | oil for frying |
| | olive oil |

Because he has settled in the area around Nice, our chef acknowledges his close association with Mediterranean culinary traditions, but because he originally comes from Alsace, he also gets nostalgic about the cornmeal soups of his childhood. He thus hit on the idea of bringing a southern flavor to what was an old Alsatian family recipe.

This soup also hints at nearby Italy, in that our chef, who has worked in Milan, uses polenta in his recipe. Many dishes from Nice use this yellow cornmeal, which is usually eaten salted. When you start preparing this dish, the polenta should always be browned with the onions in oil and/or butter. If you think the soup is too thick, just add a splash more water.

The onions give this soup its characteristic flavor. The onion is a vegetable from Asia and has been cultivated for over 5,000 years. It consists of white, fleshy leaves that are surrounded by yellow, brown, red, or white skin of a papery texture.

The polenta soup is a wonderful accompaniment to shrimp. When you buy shrimp, they should look perfect. You can tell whether they are fresh or not by how curved the shell is, how firm the flesh, and whether they are easy to shell. When you sauté the shrimp in the skillet the oil must be very hot. Depending on what's available, you could also prepare this soup with langoustines or lobster.

A pinch of hot paprika is essential to this dish. Dried *piment d'Espelette* is best. This red chile is available as a dried pepper, as a powder, or paste.

To make the garnish, peel the onion for the garnish and slice very thinly. Toss the onion rings in the flour and put aside. Wash the scallions and chop the green part into thin rings. Peel the garlic and slice it thinly. Put aside.

Peel the onion for the soup and chop it roughly. Heat 2 tbsp olive oil and a scant ⅛ stick/10 g butter in a skillet, add the onion, and sauté until golden brown, stirring occasionally.

Add the polenta and stir vigorously for 5 minutes, until the polenta has browned.

# with Polenta

Add the chicken stock and simmer for 20 minutes. Keep the soup warm. Heat the oil for frying and fry the floured onion rings. Scoop them out with a spatula and leave them to drain on kitchen paper.

Remove the heads of the shrimp. Gradually pull away the sections of shell. Open up the shrimp with the thumb and forefinger and remove the intestines.

Heat the remaining olive oil in a skillet and sauté the shrimp for about 3 minutes. Add the garlic and scallions. Season with a pinch of paprika. Arrange the shrimp in a bowl, and pour over 2 ladles of soup per bowl. Garnish with the deep-fried onion rings and a drop of olive oil.

# Vegetable Soup

Preparation time: 50 minutes
Soaking time: 12 hours
Cooking time: 50 minutes
Difficulty: ★★

**Serves 4**

| | |
|---|---|
| 2 | tomatoes |
| 5 oz/150 g | carrots |
| 3½ oz/100 g | potatoes |
| 7 oz/200 g | zucchini |
| 7 oz/200 g | green beans |
| ½ cup/100 g | dried red kidney beans |
| ½ cup/100 g | dried white kidney beans |
| 1 | onion |
| 1 clove | garlic |
| | salt, pepper |
| | fresh basil |

**For the bouquet garni:**

| | |
|---|---|
| | thyme |
| | bay leaf |
| 1 sprig | parsley |
| 2 | leek leaves |

**For the pistou:**

| | |
|---|---|
| 2 oz/50 g | garlic |
| 1 | tomato |
| 1 bunch | fresh basil |
| 4 tbsp | olive oil |

**For the baked eggplant purée:**

| | |
|---|---|
| 4 cloves | garlic |
| 2 | eggplants |
| 7 tbsp | olive oil |
| 2 sheets | phyllo (filo) pastry |

**For the tomato mousse:**

| | |
|---|---|
| 1 cup/250 ml | cream |
| 2 sachets | gelatin |
| 1 | onion |
| 2 cloves | garlic |
| 2 | tomatoes |
| 2 tbsp | olive oil |

This too is a classic Mediterranean soup, traditionally eaten hot, but when you prepare Francis Robin's recipe, you'll be pleasantly surprised how good it tastes cold. You really do need all the vegetables our chef has listed, otherwise it's not a real *soupe au pistou*. Cut the vegetables into even-sized pieces, so they cook at the same speed.

If you can, buy the best quality red and white kidney beans (available from June to September in southeastern France and in Italy). Soak them separately, if possible overnight, so they will cook more quickly. When cooking them, don't salt the water to start with, otherwise the beans will become tough and won't cook properly. Only add salt to the soup once the beans are cooked. Use young, firm zucchini and carrots, because they taste best.

Basil crushed in a mortar is called *pistou* in Provençal. Take the basil out of the refrigerator at the last minute and don't rinse the leaves, otherwise they lose their powerful scent and flavor.

The gelatin helps the tomato mousse to hold its shape. Soften it in lukewarm water in advance, according to the manufacturer's instructions, and then let it melt in hot olive oil. If you want the mousse to be a bit redder, add a teaspoon of tomato paste. The best tomatoes to use are ripe, juicy plum tomatoes. The eggplant patty is placed on top of the soup once it has cooled down a bit, so that it doesn't become soggy too quickly.

Put the tomatoes in a bowl and pour boiling water over them. Leave them for a few minutes, drain, and skin them. Dice the vegetables and tomatoes. If the red and white kidneys beans are too big, cut them in half. Preheat the oven to 400 °F/200 °C.

Put 4 cups/2 l water in a saucepan with the onion, garlic, and bouquet garni, and bring to the boil. Add the beans and simmer for 20 minutes. Then add the carrots, potatoes, zucchini and, finally, the tomatoes. Simmer on low heat for 20 minutes, then season with salt and pepper.

Place 4 unpeeled cloves of garlic on a baking sheet with the halved, deseeded eggplants. Drizzle over 4 tbsp olive oil. Bake for 25 minutes. When the eggplants have cooled, remove the flesh from the skin, peel the garlic, and purée both. Add the remaining olive oil and season.

# with Pistou

For the pistou, peel the garlic. Skin and deseed the tomato. Put the garlic and tomatoes in a food processor with the basil and olive oil, and purée them. Season to taste. Take the soup off the burner, remove the bouquet garni, and add the pistou to thicken it.

Beat the cream until stiff and reserve it. Dissolve the gelatin in lukewarm water. Cut 8 phyllo circles, 2½–3 in/6–8 cm in diameter. Put a teaspoon of eggplant purée onto 4 of the pastry circles and cover with the other 4 circles. Crimp the edges, and bake for 10 minutes at 400 °F/200 °C.

Chop and fry the onion, garlic and tomatoes until very soft. Purée the mixture. Melt the softened gelatin in hot oil. Fold the gelatin and cream into the tomato purée. Place an eggplant purée patty on top of each plate of soup, and garnish with tomato mousse and basil.

# Broccoli Soup with

Preparation time: 25 minutes
Cooking time: 35 minutes
Difficulty: ★

**Serves 4**

| | |
|---|---|
| 4 | langoustines, each 3½ oz/100 g |
| 2 tsp/10 g | sesame seeds |
| 3 tbsp | olive oil |
| | salt |
| | pepper |
| 6 | large oysters |

| | |
|---|---|
| generous 1½ lb/ 800 g | broccoli |
| 1 clove | garlic |
| 1 | shallot |
| 1 | white onion |
| 2 cups/500 ml | chicken stock |
| 7 oz/200 g | chanterelle mushrooms |
| 1 head | white cabbage weighing 10 oz/300 g |

**For the garnish:**

| | |
|---|---|
| 1 tbsp | light cream |
| 12 | broccoli florets |

Broccoli soup with white cabbage roulades and langoustines is a great winter dish. In the countryside behind Nice, the appearance of chanterelle mushrooms, used in this dish, herald the first snows of winter. The iodine-containing oysters lend this dish their invigorating aroma.

The white cabbage used in this recipe is a little less complicated to prepare than other varieties, such as green cabbage. After you have cut away the stalk you can pull off the leaves. Cut them in half lengthwise and remove the spine. When you blanch the cabbage leaves, refresh them in ice water immediately and then leave them to drain on kitchen paper. If you prefer to use green cabbage, use the palest leaves. Place them between two sheets of plastic film and beat them until they are transparent.

Broccoli is a relative of cauliflower, which you can use instead. With its flowery heads and thick stalk, broccoli is served like asparagus, or as an accompaniment to a fish or meat dish.

Don't add too much pepper to the soup. Green vegetables tend to absorb pepper. The same applies to salt. Oysters contain a lot of iodine. These delicate shellfish must be stored in a cool, dark place at a temperature between 41 and 59 degrees Fahrenheit (5 and 15 degrees Celsius).

The langoustines should be very shiny and have very bright, black eyes. Sautéing them with the sesame seeds gives them a flavor of hazelnuts and almonds. You could use spelt flour instead.

Depending on the time of year and what is available, our chef recommends you use chanterelles or boletus mushrooms (porcini).

Shell the langoustines and insert a toothpick lengthwise through the body. Roll the langoustines in sesame seeds in a dish. Heat 1 tbsp olive oil and sauté them for 2 minutes on each side over medium heat. Season to taste. When they have cooled, remove the toothpick.

Open the oysters and pour the contents into a pan. Bring the oysters to the boil. Cut the broccoli into florets. Bring a saucepan of salted water to the boil, add 12 broccoli florets and cook them for 5 minutes. Drain them, blanch in cold water, and put them aside for the garnish.

Sweat the remaining broccoli florets in a saucepan with 1 tbsp olive oil. Add the chopped garlic, shallot, and onion, then the chicken stock and 2 cups/500 ml water. Season the soup and simmer for 15 minutes, then purée it in a processor, or in the saucepan with a hand blender.

# White Cabbage Roulades

Wash the chanterelle mushrooms, drain, and cut off the stalks. Heat 1 tbsp olive oil in a skillet and sauté them. Deglaze the pan with the oyster liquor. Add the drained oysters to the pan. Season to taste. Remove the leaves from the cabbage, blanch the leaves for 6 minutes.

Put half a cabbage leaf on a sheet of plastic wrap. Put a little of the mushroom mixture and an oyster on top of the leaf. Draw up the plastic wrap around the cabbage leaf and filling and shape it into a little roll. Leave to rest for 5 minutes.

Pour the soup into bowls. Take the plastic wrap from around the cabbage roulades and put one in the center of the soup. Arrange a langoustine either side of the cabbage roulade. Finally add the cooked broccoli florets and a spoonful of light cream.

# Fish &
# Seafood

# One-pot Stew with

Preparation time:   30 minutes
Cooking time:       1 hour 15 minutes
Difficulty:         ★

**Serves 4**

| | |
|---|---|
| 4 | potatoes |
| | saffron threads |
| 2¼ lb/1 kg | baby squid |
| 1 tbsp | olive oil |
| 1 cup/250 ml | fish stock |
| 1 cup/250 ml | light cream |
| | salt |
| | pepper |

**For the sofregit:**

| | |
|---|---|
| 1 clove | garlic |
| 1 | onion |
| 2 oz slab/50 g | back bacon |
| | (or Catalan *sagi*) |

**For the aioli (garlic mayonnaise):**

| | |
|---|---|
| 1 clove | garlic, unpeeled |
| 1 | egg yolk |
| 6 tbsp | olive oil |
| | salt |

The boats of Catalan fishermen rock against their moorings on the Mediterranean's gentle waves. We are in Port-Vendres... it was a good catch and it's all been sold. Now all that remains is to prepare the delicious baby squid, or very small cuttlefish (*supions*), which are similar. With them the fisherman fry up *sagi*, a rancid white bacon that gives a nutty flavor, especially in the traditional *bullinada de supions*. You can replace the *sagi* in our recipe with regular bacon, or a good olive oil.

Jean Plouzennec's recipe can be served as an appetizer, but you should use more squid. If you can't obtain baby squid or very small cuttlefish, you can use squid rings. *Sofregit*, one of the basic recipes of Catalan cuisine, forms the basis of this dish, with its caramelized onions and sometimes tomatoes as well. The precise ingredients vary from family to family.

*Bullinada* is served with *aioli*, a strong garlic mayonnaise extremely popular in southern French cuisine. All of the ingredients must be at the same temperature for it to be successful. Our chef suggests that you put in the salt at the beginning.

You need the best garlic that you can find for *aioli*. You can use the white or the pink variety. Your dressing will have the best flavor if the bulbs are young, and you have removed the cores from the cloves. The garlic should be crushed well. Sweated, soft garlic is also easier to work.

The olive oil should be perfumed and slightly cloudy; if it is, the *aioli* will taste even better! We're less demanding about the variety of potato, also an integral part of *bullinada*, but you should definitely use a waxy variety.

*To make the sofregit, peel the garlic and onion and chop them finely. Chop the bacon finely too. Put half the bacon in a deep saucepan and fry it until the fat runs. Then fry the garlic and onion in the bacon fat. Put aside the remaining chopped bacon for the next step.*

*Peel the potatoes and slice them into ¼ in/3 mm-thick slices. Put the potatoes in a pan of boiling, salted water, adding the remaining bacon and 10 strands of saffron. Simmer for 15 minutes, then drain the potatoes, reserving 1 tbsp potato liquor. Add a little pepper.*

*Clean and gut the squid and squeeze them gently to remove excess moisture. Fry all the squid and tentacles in olive oil in a skillet for 2 minutes until all the liquid has evaporated and the squid is pale golden brown.*

# Baby Squid and Bacon

Add the browned squid to the pan with the onion, garlic, and bacon. Add the fish stock and sprinkle on some saffron. Bring to the boil. Add the cream. Bring to the boil again. Simmer for 45 minutes.

To make the aioli, roast one clove of garlic in the oven, peel it, and crush it with salt and the egg yolk. As with a mayonnaise, using a wire whisk, beat in the olive oil. Add 1 tbsp potato liquor.

Add the aioli to the pan with the squid. Stir to form a smooth mixture. Arrange a circle of potato slices around the edge of the plate. Pour the squid into the middle and serve immediately.

# Baked Porgy

Preparation time: 30 minutes
Cooking time: 40 minutes
Difficulty: ✷

**Serves 4**

| | |
|---|---|
| 2 | large onions |
| 3 cloves | garlic |
| 7 tbsp | olive oil |
| 1 sprig | fresh or dried dill |

| | |
|---|---|
| 1 | porgy weighing 2¼ lb/1 kg |
| 8 | medium new potatoes |
| 1 tbsp | chopped fresh thyme |
| 2 | bay leaves |
| 4 | tomatoes |
| 2 | lemons |
| ⅔ cup/150 ml | dry white wine |
| | salt |
| | pepper |

Here is a dish that is one of the most popular Sunday meals among families in southern France, and it is one of the easiest fish recipes ever. To make preparation even easier, ask your fishmonger to scale, gut, and clean the porgy for you. This fish is easy to identify because of the pale stripes on its cheeks.

Our dish is seasonal. Porgy is only available between March and October. If you can't find it, use bass.

The porgy's eyes should be bright and the gills red, signs that the fish is fresh. Take care not to cook it for too long, otherwise it will become dry. Here's a gourmet tip: This dish tastes even better the next day. The potatoes will have soaked up the delicious juices – a fantastic treat for the taste buds – and the flavors will have married perfectly.

We decided to use new potatoes for this dish because they are well suited to baking in the oven. You could use other kinds of potato, though. Whilst in the oven the fish must be well covered from head to tail, otherwise it will burn.

The splendid porgy is easy to prepare and eat, because it doesn't have too many bones. Even novice cooks will enjoy this recipe. It's so simple that nothing can go wrong. The red tomatoes and yellow lemons are all that is needed by way of a garnish. The fish is the star.

Sauté the sliced onions and garlic in 2 tbsp olive oil until golden brown. Put the onions and garlic in an oven-proof dish large enough to take the porgy.

Insert the sprig of fresh or dried dill into the prepared porgy's belly cavity. Drizzle 1 tbsp oil over the porgy.

Cut the peeled potatoes into ¼ in/5 mm-thick slices. Sauté them in olive oil, with 1 tbsp chopped thyme and 2 bay leaves, until golden brown. Season with salt.

# with Vegetables

Layer the fried potato on top of the onion and garlic in the oven-proof dish. Arrange the tomatoes, sliced into ¼ in/5 mm-thick slices, and the lemon slices, on top, putting some aside for later.

Put the porgy on top of the vegetables and garnish with slices of lemon and tomato. Season with salt and pepper and drizzle the remaining olive oil over the fish.

Pour the white wine over the fish and vegetables. Cover with aluminum foil and bake for 30 minutes in an oven preheated to 400 °F/200 °C, basting every 5 minutes with the cooking juices. Serve hot, straight from the dish.

# Fillet of Sea Bass

Preparation time: 40 minutes
Cooking time: 30 minutes
Difficulty: ★

**Serves 4**

| | |
|---|---|
| 2¼ lb/1 kg | sea bass |
| 15 | baby carrots |
| 2 | zucchini |
| 1 tbsp | olive oil |
| | salt |
| | pepper |

**For the fish stock:**

| | |
|---|---|
| | sea bass trimmings |
| 3 tbsp | olive oil |

| | |
|---|---|
| 1 | leek |
| 1 | onion |
| 1 bunch | fresh parsley |
| 1 sprig | fresh thyme |
| 1 | bay leaf |
| ⅓ cup + 1½ tbsp/ 100 ml | white wine |
| 6 tsp | aniseed seeds |

**For the zabaglione:**

| | |
|---|---|
| 3 | egg yolks |
| ⅓ cup + 1½ tbsp/ 100 ml | light cream |

**For the garnish:**

| | |
|---|---|
| 1 bunch | fresh chervil |

Sea bass is a member of the serranid family and is an extremely popular edible fish. Get your fishmonger to fillet it for you if possible, but ask him to save you the bones and head, minus the gills, because you need them for the fish stock. Wash the fish carefully and, above all, do not salt it. Depending on the time of year, you can substitute porgy or John Dory.

Zabaglione is really an Italian dessert. In this dish it is served hot. Our chef advises that you move it to the edge of the burner when you beat it, so that it doesn't go lumpy. The zabaglione will remain liquid if you don't add the cream until the end. Purée the sauce in a blender and then strain it through a sieve to remove the aniseeds. Just before serving, pour enough zabaglione into the base of an oven-proof plate to cover it, and bake it in the oven for two minutes at 465 degrees Fahrenheit/250 degrees Celsius, so that the sauce turns golden brown.

Aniseed originated in the Orient and is a member of the umbelliferous plant family. In ancient China, aniseed was regarded as a holy herb and the Romans valued it too. In Europe, aniseeds were used in baking from the earliest times. For this recipe you could use fennel seeds instead.

Our chef cooks the carrots first, then the zucchini. Briefly blanch the vegetables in cold water afterwards, so that they retain their attractive color. You could make a soup with the remaining vegetables.

Use a griddle to broil the fish fillets. The ridges make an attractive pattern on the fish. You can serve boiled potatoes with this dish.

*Make an incision in the fish along the backbone, from head to tail, and then make another incision behind the gills. Cut off the full length of the fillet by working the knife along the length of the fish against the backbone. Remove the second fillet in the same way.*

*Fish stock: Put the fish bones, fish head, and olive oil in a saucepan. Add a little water, followed by the washed and chopped leek, chopped onion and parsley, thyme, and bay leaf. Simmer for 10 minutes. Add the white wine. Simmer for 10 minutes, then sprinkle in the aniseeds.*

*Starting at the tail, cut the fish fillets into equal chunks, then refrigerate them. Slice the carrots and zucchini on the diagonal to form oval slices and boil them (carrots first, see above) for 5 minutes in salted water.*

# on Aniseed Zabaglione

To make the zabaglione, strain the fish stock and beat in the egg yolks.

Beat the egg yolks hard with a wire whisk over heat so that the mixture thickens.

Add the cream and season to taste. Purée the zabaglione on the highest setting, so that it emulsifies, and strain. Fry the fish for 5 minutes in 1 tbsp olive oil. Season the sea bass with salt. Arrange the zabaglione sauce, fish and vegetables on a plate. Garnish with chervil.

# Fideus in Cuttlefish Ink

Preparation time:   45 minutes
Cooking time:       1 hour 50 minutes
Difficulty:         ★

**Serves 4**

| | |
|---|---|
| 1 lb/500 g | cuttlefish with ink |
| 1 | small leek |
| 1 | onion |
| 1 sprig | fresh thyme |
| 1 | bay leaf |
| 4 | langoustines, shelled and deveined |
| 1 | sweet onion |
| 2 cloves | garlic |

| | |
|---|---|
| 1 tbsp | olive oil |
| 1 | potato |
| 10 oz/300 g | thick fresh noodles |

| | |
|---|---|
| | oil for frying |
| | salt |

**For the crab sauce:**

| | |
|---|---|
| 6 | small spider crabs |
| 3 tbsp | olive oil |
| 1 | white onion |
| 3 cloves | garlic |
| 1 sprig | fresh thyme |
| ⅓ cup + 1½ tbsp/ 100 ml | Banyuls (or other fortified sweet wine) |
| generous ¾ stick/100 g | butter |
| | salt, pepper |

*Fideus* (Catalan thick noodles) in cuttlefish ink with langoustines, is a specialty of the beach resorts of Collioure and Port-Vendres. This dish from the Roussillon coast was originally prepared in large earthenware dishes, in which the cuttlefish was cooked for one and a half hours with thyme, bay leaf, and onions. Then the fishermen added the *fideus*. Because these noodles are usually only available locally, you could use spaghetti instead, breaking it up into short lengths.

The cuttlefish (sepia) from the seas around the Mediterranean coast is around 12 inches/30 centimeters long. Depending on the area, it is known as *supion*, *sépia*, or *margate*. The ink is used in many dishes. If cuttlefish is not available, you could use squid or octopus instead. If you use octopus, you must beat it with a meat tenderizer. The ink is also sold separately in vacuum-packed bags.

The langoustine gives this traditional dish a certain style. This wonderful crustacean, with its rose-pink shell, is available between April and August. When you peel the langoustines make sure you keep the heads and pincers whole for use as a garnish. Devein the langoustines and make a small cut in the belly to make it easier to sauté them, because they have a tendency to curl up when cooked. To help them keep their shape, you can pierce them lengthways with a toothpick, which should be removed before serving. If you can't find langoustines, you could use large shrimp instead. The spider crabs, used to form the basis of the sauce, can be replaced by dwarf swimming crabs.

*Fideus* in cuttlefish ink with langoustines helps bring the maritime freshness of the Catalan Mediterranean coast to your plate.

---

*Clean and prepare the cuttlefish. Put the halved cuttlefish, finely chopped leek, quartered onion, sprig of thyme, and bay leaf in a saucepan. Cover with water, season with salt and bring to the boil. Cover the pan, and simmer for 1 hour. Strain the liquor, reserving it for the noodles.*

*To make the crab sauce, grasp the crab claws firmly with one hand and crack them with the other. Fry the crabs in olive oil with the chopped onion until golden brown. Season with salt and pepper. Add the chopped garlic and thyme, and continue cooking.*

*Deglaze the crabs with the Banyuls. Simmer for 20 minutes. Add the langoustine heads and simmer for 10 minutes with lid on. Remove the heads for the garnish. Purée the crab mixture and strain it. Return the sauce to the pan and reduce it for 3 minutes. Beat in the butter.*

# with Langoustines

Fry the finely chopped sweet onion and chopped garlic in the olive oil.

Coat the shelled langoustines in the peeled and finely grated potato. Fry them gently in hot oil and put them aside. Put the noodles, or spaghetti, in the pan with the onions and garlic.

Pour the fish broth over the noodles. Add 1 tsp cuttlefish ink and simmer for 20 minutes. Cut some of the cuttlefish into 12 slices and dice the rest. Arrange all the cuttlefish, with langoustines, on a bed of black noodles. Pour the crab sauce over the noodles and cuttlefish.

# Red Mullet Fillets

| | |
|---|---|
| Preparation time: | *2 hours* |
| Cooking time: | *45 minutes* |
| Difficulty: | ★★★ |

**Serves 4**

| | |
|---|---|
| 4 | red mullet, each 8 oz/250 g |
| 1 tbsp | olive oil |
| 1 bunch | fresh dill |
| | salt, pepper |

**For the fish soup:**

| | |
|---|---|
| 1 | onion |
| 1 | carrot |
| 1 clove | garlic |
| 1 | bouquet garni |
| 2 tbsp | olive oil |
| 1 lb/500 g | assorted rock fish |
| generous ¾ cup/200 ml | Pernod/aniseed drink |
| 1 sprig | fresh dill |
| 1 large pinch | ground saffron |
| 2 tbsp | tomato paste |
| | salt, pepper |

**For the ratatouille:**

| | |
|---|---|
| 2 | zucchini |
| 1 | large eggplant |
| 1 | onion |
| 1 clove | garlic |
| 1 | red bell pepper |
| 1 | green bell pepper |
| 2 tbsp | olive oil |
| 1 sprig | fresh thyme (optional) |
| | salt, pepper |

**For the red garlic mayonnaise (rouille):**

| | |
|---|---|
| 1 | egg yolk |
| 1 tsp | Dijon/mild mustard (optional) |
| generous ¾ cup/200 ml | olive oil |
| 1 pinch | ground saffron |
| 1 pinch | harissa/chilli powder, salt |

This recipe is a complete homage to the south of France! Alain Carro has given this creation the same name as his restaurant, "Le Castellaras," after the prehistoric fortifications on the peaks of the Maritime Alps. If you visit this area, take a little time before you eat to enjoy a traditional aperitif in the form of the aniseed alcoholic drink, *pastis.*

All of the ingredients in this recipe come from an area that basks in the sun. It is an extremely refined dish, both in taste and presentation. For this specialty to be a total success, the ratatouille vegetables should be chopped into fine dice, as it is important for the finished appearance.

Remove the bell pepper cores and chop all the vegetables into evenly sized dice. Get your fishmonger to fillet the red mullet (red snapper can be used if red mullet is unavailable). If you want to make the effort yourself, clean and gut the fish carefully and fillet it with a sharp knife. Don't forget to remove the smallest bones with a pair of tweezers. Rock fish don't need to be gutted and filleted, they just need to be rinsed well. The small fish should be very fresh.

You'll recognize them all again – the little green and black striped white sea bream, the green and brown hog fish, the delicate, long, red and black striped rainbow wrasse, the red and green spotted bass, and the scorpion fish. When the catch is exceptional, the fisherman may sometimes find small crustaceans in his nets, known as rock lobster (*cigalons de mer*).

*Rouille* is based on a simple mayonnaise. To help it emulsify, add a small teaspoon of mustard or a splash of water. This will also help if the mayonnaise separates.

*Peel and dice the onion, carrot, and garlic for the soup. Add the bouquet garni and sweat everything in the olive oil.*

*When the onions are translucent, add the rock fish to the pan and sauté them too.*

*Add the aniseed drink, sprig of dill, saffron, and tomato paste. Add enough water to cover the ingredients. Simmer for 20 minutes. Season the soup. Remove the dill and bouquet garni from the pan. Pour the soup into a food processor, purée it, then pass it through a sieve.*

# "Castellaras"

To make the ratatouille, dice the zucchini, eggplant, onion, garlic, and bell peppers very finely. Sweat them in the olive oil for 10 minutes until the onion is translucent. The vegetables should still be crisp. Add the thyme (if using). Season with salt and pepper.

To make the garlic mayonnaise, beat together the egg yolk, mustard, and olive oil until creamy. Beat in the saffron, harissa powder, and salt.

Season the red mullet fillets. Fry in olive oil for 2 minutes on the skin side and 3 minutes on the flesh side. Sandwich the ratatouille between two fillets. Make a pool of soup around the fish. Put a spoonful of rouille in the soup. Garnish with sprigs of fresh dill.

# Red Mullet with

Preparation time: 20 minutes
Cooking time: 10 minutes
Difficulty: ★

**Serves 4**

1½ lb/800 g  red mullet fillets
4 tbsp  olive oil
salt
pepper

**For the anchovy sauce (pissalat):**
1 cup/200 g  small black olives
2 oz/50 g  anchovy fillets in oil

⅓ cup + 1½ tbsp/
100 ml  olive oil
8 tbsp  fish stock
⅓ cup + 1½ tbsp/
100 ml  light cream
¼ stick/30 g  butter
8  cherry tomatoes
salt
pepper

**For the garnish:**
fresh chervil

Red mullet are found both in the Mediterranean Sea and the Atlantic Ocean. This small, reddish fish is a bit bigger than a sardine. It is easily recognizable because of the barbels hanging down either side of its mouth. Fall is the best time of year to enjoy red mullet. It is the traditional main ingredient for this dish, and is used in Europe.

In this recipe, you can also use red snapper, which is just as tasty. If you can't find it, you could use sea bass or porgy instead. Whatever the fish you choose, when you buy it, make sure that the gills are pink or red and the whole fish looks "lively."

To make it easier to prepare this dish, ask your fishmonger to fillet the fish. If you take out the bones, run your finger over the fish repeatedly. If the fish feels uneven, there are still bones in it. For the other important ingredient in our recipe, the anchovy sauce known as *pissalat*, Jean-Michel

Minguella uses flavorful Niçoise olives, exclusively from the area around Nice. They have an elegant, elongated shape and are quite small. They are not only prized by our chef, they are also regarded as the best for making olive oil. Their flavor, with the characteristic hint of acidity, emphasizes the taste of the red mullet or red snapper. You could, of course, use other types of black olive. If you buy pitted olives, you'll be saving yourself some time.

To heighten the taste of the anchovy sauce, we recommend flavoring it with thyme and bay leaf. Before finishing the dish with the *pissalat*, heat it briefly in the oven, so it's nice and smooth.

*Clean and gut the red mullet. Fillet the fish by running a knife along the backbone from tail to head. Remove any remaining bones using a pair of tweezers. Season the fillets with salt and pepper.*

*To make the anchovy sauce, purée ⅓ cup/60 g pitted olives in a food processor with the anchovies. Add the olive oil.*

*Pass the anchovy and olive mixture through a sieve, stir in the fish stock, and reserve the sauce.*

# Anchovy Sauce

Preheat the oven to 430 °F/220 °C. Gently heat the cream in a saucepan, add the butter, and beat it into the sauce. Set the sauce to one side.

Fold the olive and anchovy mixture into the cream. Burn a diamond pattern on the skin side of the fish fillets using a very hot broiler rack. Put the red mullet fillets flesh side down on an oiled baking sheet, and season them. Cooking time depends on the thickness of the fish fillets.

Bake the remaining olives and the cherry tomatoes in olive oil for 5 minutes. Arrange the fillets on warmed plates. Dot the anchovy sauce around the fish fillets and garnish them with the olives and tomatoes. Drizzle a little olive oil over the fish and garnish with fresh chervil.

# Monkfish with a

Preparation time: 30 minutes
Vegetable cooking time: 30 minutes
Monkfish cooking time: 15 minutes
Difficulty: ★★

**Serves 4**

| | |
|---|---|
| 2 | monkfish tails weighing 1½ lb/800 g |
| 8 | baby carrots |
| 4 | potatoes |
| 8 | baby turnips |
| 4 bulbs | baby fennel |
| 7 cloves | garlic |
| 2 | bay leaves |
| 10 slices | white bread |

| | |
|---|---|
| 1 bunch | fresh parsley |
| ½ bunch | fresh thyme |

| | |
|---|---|
| | salt |
| | pepper |
| 2 | eggs |
| 2 tbsp | olive oil |
| 7 tbsp | peanut oil |
| scant ⅛ stick/10 g | butter |
| 1 cup/100 g | pitted black olives |

**For the garlic mayonnaise (aioli):**

| | |
|---|---|
| 4 cloves | garlic |
| 1 | egg yolk |
| 1 cup/ 250 ml | olive oil |
| 1 pinch | saffron |
| | salt |

In this recipe by Francis Robin, the tender, delicate flesh of the monkfish is dressed in a golden robe, which gives it an incomparable flavor. This fish is easy to prepare and also very suitable for children, because the fish only has one large backbone. Fishmongers often sell it in pieces, but it is rarely displayed with the head. When choosing monkfish, the flesh should be snow white. If you can see yellow fibers, choose another, fresher fish.

The unusual thing about this dish is that it looks like a leg of lamb, spiked with slivers of garlic. In fact, garlic is used in every Mediterranean dish. *Aioli*, the special mayonnaise from the south of France, is an integral part of our recipe, and garlic is the main ingredient in it. To ensure that your garlic mayonnaise is a success, we recommend crushing the garlic, then salting it. Only then should you add the egg yolk and very gradually beat in the olive oil, a drop at a time.

The vegetable accompaniment should have a very subtle taste. Francis Robin therefore recommends that you omit tomatoes, eggplant, and zucchini. Use waxy potatoes, such as Charlotte, that don't break down when cooked.

Normal vegetables can of course be used instead of the baby vegetables. Buy fennel that is white and plump, with a nice, bright green stalk, but try to get small bulbs, because they are sweeter than the big ones. Fennel will keep for several days in the refrigerator. The carrots and baby turnips should have smooth, shiny skins.

*Clean the monkfish tails, removing any skin and fat. Peel the carrots, potatoes, baby turnips, and fennel, leaving a little bit of stalk on the carrots and baby turnips. Cook each vegetable separately in boiling salted water, with a clove of garlic and half a bay leaf.*

*A day in advance, pass the bread through a wide-meshed sieve to make breadcrumbs, and leave them uncovered, to dry. Put the breadcrumbs into a bowl. Stir in 4 chopped cloves of garlic, chopped fresh parsley and thyme. Season with salt and pepper.*

*Peel 2 cloves of garlic, cut them into slivers, and insert them all over the monkfish tails. Beat together the eggs and olive oil.*

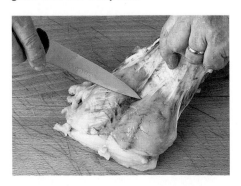

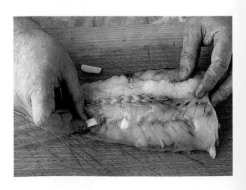

# Herb Crust

Dip the monkfish tails in the beaten egg, then coat them in the herbed bread-crumbs. To make the aioli, crush the peeled garlic in a mortar. Season with salt and add the egg yolk. Gradually beat in the olive oil and a pinch of saffron.

Preheat the oven to 400 °F/200 °C. Melt the peanut oil and butter in a large, oven-proof skillet. Fry the fish in the butter and oil until crisp and golden brown. Then transfer the pan to the oven and bake for 10 minutes.

Keep an eye on the baking fish, basting it frequently with cooking juices. Arrange the vegetables and olives around the fish, and serve the aioli separately.

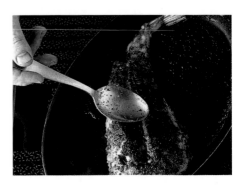

# Spiny Lobster

Preparation time: 40 minutes
Cooking time: 50 minutes
Difficulty: ★★

**Serves 4**

| | |
|---|---|
| 1 | spiny lobster weighing 3½ lb/1.5 kg |
| 2 tbsp | olive oil |
| ⅓ cup + 1½ tbsp/ 100 ml | dry Banyuls |
| 1–2 squares/ 10 g | semisweet chocolate |
| scant ¼ stick/ 20 g | butter, chilled |
| 1 | globe artichoke |

oil for frying
salt, pepper

**For the fish stock:**

| | |
|---|---|
| 1 | carrot |
| 1 | onion |
| 4 cloves | garlic |
| 2 | anchovies |
| 1 tbsp | olive oil |
| | zest of 2 unwaxed oranges |

**For the bouquet garni:**

| | |
|---|---|
| 1 stick | celery |
| | fresh thyme |
| 1 | bay leaf |
| 1 bunch | fresh parsley |

For this dish, which is served in Catalonia at big celebrations, you need a lobster of "royale" quality, from the Mediterranean Sea. Spiny lobsters are often sold alive, which isn't to everyone's taste, because you then have to dispatch the crustaceans before preparing them. In many countries this is done by one carefully placed stab to the head. We, however, prefer to dispatch them in boiling water. The water must be at a rolling boil so that the end comes as quickly as possible, and the creatures must be put into the water head first. This is why we often use lobsters that are ready to cook, or simply use the shelled tail meat. If you don't want to dispatch the lobster, buy one that is ready to cook, but has not yet been dressed.

This dish uses a stock flavored with carrot, onion, garlic, a bouquet garni, and a tablespoon of olive oil. You also need the liquor from the orange zest, which should be boiled in ⅔ cup/150 milliliters water. The lobster head is cooked in this orange-flavored stock. If preferred, you can use ⅔ cup/150 milliliters ready-made fish stock instead of preparing the stock as described in step one of the method.

Jean Plouzennec's recipe is based on the traditional method of preparing Catalan chocolate lobster. Chocolate is used frequently in recipes from this region. This complements the sweet and salty flavor of the dish. Not far from Amélie-les-Bains, where our head chef lives, the former ancient spice route runs through Port-Vendres. Even today, Catalan cuisine makes much use of chocolate, cinnamon, saffron, and many other classic spices.

Banyuls is a sweet, fortified dessert wine. It bears the name of the place where it originated, but is also produced in Collioure, Cerbère, and Port-Vendres. It is available as a "grand cru" and "dry" or "brut," also called "sec." If you cannot find Banyuls, use another fortified wine.

*Fry the diced carrot, onion, and garlic in olive oil for 5 minutes. Add the soaked, chopped anchovy fillets, the liquor from the boiled orange zest (see above), and the chopped bouquet garni ingredients. Simmer the lobster head for 20 minutes. Strain the fish stock and put aside.*

*Halve the spiny lobster, rinse and pat dry. Using an oven-proof skillet, fry the lobster halves in olive oil for 3 minutes on each side, starting with the flesh side.*

*Preheat the oven to 400 °F/200 °C. Deglaze the lobster with the Banyuls wine, or other fortified wine. Bake the lobster in the oven for 15 minutes.*

# à la Banyulaise

Boil the fish stock until reduced by one quarter. Add the semisweet chocolate. Turn up the burner and beat in the chilled butter, a small piece at a time. Strain the sauce and put aside.

Before serving, season the chocolate sauce to taste with salt and pepper. Pour the chocolate sauce over the baked lobster when it comes out of the oven.

While the lobster is in the oven, clean the artichoke and slice the heart into thin chips using a vegetable peeler or mandolin cutter. Heat the oil and fry the artichoke chips in it until golden brown. Drain and reserve them. Garnish the lobster with the artichoke chips.

# Red Mullet on a

Preparation time:    10 minutes
Cooking time:        10 minutes
Difficulty:          ★

**Serves 4**

| | |
|---|---|
| 4 | plum tomatoes |
| 3 tbsp | olive oil |
| 2 | shallots |
| 1 clove | garlic |
| 1 cup/100 g | pitted black olives |

| | |
|---|---|
| 4 | red mullet, each |
| | 8 oz/250 g, filleted |
| | salt |
| | pepper |

**For the balsamic vinaigrette:**

| | |
|---|---|
| 1 tbsp | balsamic vinegar |
| 3 tbsp | olive oil |
| | salt |
| | pepper |

Christian Étienne is very fond of Provence, where he was born and grew up. The restaurant that bears his name is located in the center of Avignon, beside the Pope's Palace, and the building once belonged to the Papal Vice-Legate. Inside the restaurant, 15th-century frescoes are a reminder of these splendors.

Red mullet from the Mediterranean Sea is prized above all for its delicate flesh, which is tender and yet firm. In this recipe, you can use red snapper instead, or you could use monkfish or cod. Ask for the fish to be filleted for you.

In summer, the chef's menu revolves around tomatoes. Tomatoes came from Peru originally. They were imported to Spain in the 16th century, where they were regarded initially as poisonous. It took almost 200 years for tomatoes to be common on the tables of Europe.

Roma, a variety of plum tomato, is also known by the name *olivette*. Plum tomatoes are cultivated mainly in Provence and Languedoc-Roussillon, and they are available between July and October. When you buy them, the flesh should be firm, the skin shiny, and they should be a uniform color. You can use other varieties of tomato, but they must be able to withstand frying in very hot oil.

Christian Étienne never fails to use garlic, and he gives the place of honor in this recipe to shallots. This relative of onion and garlic gives the tomatoes a fine flavor.

You could serve rice with the red mullet, or potato mashed with olive oil.

*Wash the tomatoes and cut them into slices ¼–½ in/1 cm thick.*

*Fry the tomatoes in 2 tbsp hot olive oil for 2 minutes.*

*Peel the shallots and garlic and chop them finely. Sprinkle them over the tomatoes and sweat them briefly. Season with salt and pepper, turn off the burner, and leave the tomatoes to infuse.*

# Bed of Pan-fried Tomatoes

Coarsely chop the black olives. To make the balsamic vinaigrette, beat together the salt, pepper, and balsamic vinegar. Beat in the olive oil, then add the chopped olives.

Using a spatula, lift the tomato slices out of the skillet and arrange them on a plate. Season the red mullet fillets with salt and pepper.

Fry the red mullet fillets in the remaining olive oil for 2 minutes on the skin side and 1 minute on the flesh side. Arrange the red mullet fillets on the bed of tomatoes, and dress them with the balsamic vinaigrette with olives.

# Sea Bass

Preparation time: 30 minutes
Cooking time: 30 minutes
Difficulty: ★

**Serves 4**

| | |
|---|---|
| 3½ lb/1.5 kg | sea bass |
| 2 bulbs | fennel |
| 5 tbsp | olive oil |
| 2 cups/500 ml | fish stock (see below for how to make it) |
| | salt |
| | pepper |

**For the garnish:**

| | |
|---|---|
| | fennel tops |
| 1 pinch | saffron strands |

Sea bass on braised fennel with saffron-scented fish sauce is one of the classics of Provençal cuisine. This fish is a member of the serranid family and is prized above all for its fine, firm flesh that contains little fat and tastes delicious. You could use red mullet, red snapper, cod, or monkfish instead.

If you find it difficult to fillet fish, ask for the fish to be filleted for you when you buy them. Try to get a large fish with skin, because this browns slowly during frying.

The fish stock is prepared as follows: Sweat a finely chopped onion in 1 tablespoon of olive oil. Then add 1 tablespoon of tomato paste and cook everything for one minute so that the acidic flavor of the tomato paste softens. Then add 2¼ pounds/1 kilogram of rock fish that have been cleaned and gutted, as well as any fish trimmings from the sea bass (see main method, below). Peel a bulb of garlic, crush the cloves, and add them to the fish. Season the fish

well. Add enough water to cover, 1 scant ounce/20 grams saffron strands, a sprig of thyme, and a bay leaf. Simmer the stock ingredients for 20 minutes, then strain the stock back into a pan. Continue to boil the stock until it turns syrupy, then beat in 3 tablespoons of olive oil.

As an ingredient, fennel is just as important as the fish stock. Its aniseed flavor is a wonderful accompaniment to fish. Fennel is a wide bulb of tightly packed leaves and is eaten as a vegetable. When you buy it, it should be firm and white, well rounded, with no blemishes.

The sea bass with braised fennel and saffron-scented fish sauce develops a delicate flavor of the sea in combination with a fresh aroma.

*Scale and fillet the fish. To do this, position the knife at gill height and work backwards from the head along the stomach to the tail, freeing the fillet from the backbone. Remove any remaining small bones with a pair of tweezers.*

*Reserve the fish trimmings for the fish stock. Cut the fish fillets into 4 thick pieces.*

*Wash the fennel and slice it thickly, reserving the stalk.*

# on Fennel

Fry the sliced fennel in 2 tbsp olive oil for 1–2 minutes, until golden brown.

Braise the fennel in the fish stock for about 20 minutes. Drain and cut out the root. Season the stock to taste with salt and pepper.

Season the sea bass fillets with salt and pepper. Fry them in the remaining olive oil for 5 minutes on each side. Pour a pool of sauce onto the plate. Place a slice of fennel in the middle, and put a fish fillet on top. Garnish with the fennel tops and saffron strands.

# Sea Bass with

Preparation time: 45 minutes
Cooking time: 25 minutes
Difficulty: ★★

**Serves 4**

| | |
|---|---|
| 1 | sea bass, weighing 3 lb/1.2 kg |
| 2 tbsp | olive oil |
| | salt |
| | pepper |

**For the artichokes (barigoule):**

| | | | | |
|---|---|---|---|---|
| 8 | purple globe artichokes | 1 | medium onion |
| 2 tbsp | olive oil | 2 | baby carrots |
| 1 stick | celery | 1 clove | garlic |

| | |
|---|---|
| 1 regular slice/50 g | *coppa* ham |
| ⅓ cup + 1½ tbsp/ 100 ml | white wine |
| 1 cup/250 ml | chicken stock |
| 2 | tomatoes |
| ½ cup/50 g | pitted black olives |
| 1 bunch | flat leaf parsley |
| ½ stick/50 g | butter |
| | salt |
| | pepper |

Pan-fried sea bass with artichokes is a typical Provençal dish. In southern France, *barigoule* is understood to be a dish with braised and stuffed artichokes. Originally the artichokes were cut off at the base of the globe, simply drizzled with oil, and broiled. Over time, this rustic way of preparing them changed fundamentally, so that now they are stuffed with meat.

In this recipe our chef only uses purple globe artichokes (*poivrades*), with their attractive purple-green leaves. They are so tender they can be eaten raw too. You should buy artichokes with whole, tightly closed, and unblemished leaves.

To prevent the artichoke hearts oxidizing, Daniel Ettlinger suggests you put them in water acidulated with lemon juice. Don't forget to drain them before frying!

All the vegetables should be diced finely. They should be cooked in white wine, which must evaporate fully so that the acidity does not overpower the other flavors. The tomatoes should be skinned and deseeded.

*Coppa* is an Italian and Corsican ham. You could use *pancetta*, or diced salted, lightly smoked bacon instead.

Like *barigoule*, sea bass is also part of the culinary legacy of Provence. This delicious saltwater fish, also known as *bar* in Provence, has fine, firm, lean meat. You could also prepare this recipe using porgy, or grouper. If you don't want to fillet the fish yourself, ask for it to be done for you when you buy it. Pan-fried sea bass with artichokes is served in deep plates.

*Working round the artichokes with a knife, cut off the leaves until you reach the heart, leaving a piece of stalk attached. Scratch out the chokes with a spoon.*

*Fry the artichokes with 1 tbsp olive oil and season sparingly with salt. Add the finely diced celery, onion, carrots, garlic, and ham. Sweat the vegetables for 5 minutes, stirring frequently. Season to taste with pepper and salt.*

*Deglaze the pan with the white wine and simmer until the liquid has evaporated.*

# Artichokes

Add the chicken stock and simmer for around 7 minutes, depending on the size of the artichokes.

Scale the fish, if necessary, fillet it, and remove the bones. Cut the fillets into pieces and score the skin gently. Season with salt and pepper. Fry the sea bass pieces in the remaining olive oil for 4–5 minutes on each side.

Add sliced tomatoes, pitted and halved olives, and chopped parsley to the artichokes. Season with salt and pepper. To thicken the vegetable sauce, stir in the butter and 1 tbsp olive oil. Arrange the pan-fried sea bass and artichokes on a plate and drizzle with olive oil.

# Eel Ragout

Preparation time: 30 minutes
Cooking time: 25 minutes
Difficulty: ★★

**Serves 4**

| | |
|---|---|
| 3 lb/1.2 kg | eel |
| 2 oz/50 g | onions |
| 3 oz/75 g | shallots |
| 2 | tomatoes |
| 2 cloves | garlic |
| 2 tbsp | olive oil |
| ¼ cup | wheat flour |
| | salt |
| | pepper |
| | cayenne pepper |

| | |
|---|---|
| 1 cup/250 ml | white wine |
| ⅓ cup + 1½ tbsp/100 ml | fish stock |

**For the herbs:**

| | |
|---|---|
| 1 bunch | fresh chervil |
| 1 bunch | fresh chives |
| 1 bunch | fresh flat-leaf parsley |
| 1 sprig | fresh tarragon |

**For the croutons:**

| | |
|---|---|
| 4 slices | bread |
| ⅛ stick/15 g | butter |

The eel is truly a special fish. It can grow up to around 3 feet/1 meter, and its smooth body is slippery to the touch. Eels hatch in the Sargasso Sea near Bermuda, and the larvae migrate to Europe, which takes two to three years. On arrival, they swim upriver, where they reach sexual maturity. All eels are born female, then some change sex in the course of their lives. Eels swim back to the sea to return to their breeding grounds, and it is at this stage that fishermen catch them. Only female eels are sold as food.

This dish is a classic from the Sète region, close to the Thau Basin, where eels are plentiful. Because they spoil quickly they are sold very fresh and the skin removed at the last minute. You should consume the eel on the day of purchase. Ask your fishmonger to prepare the eel for you, because it's laborious work. At least the spine can be removed with a single incision. If you buy pre-skinned and

pre-cleaned eel, you need to check how fresh it is. Eel is also available frozen, jellied in cans, or smoked.

In ancient times the Romans regarded eel as a delicacy and the epitome of refined taste, which is why they were often served at splendid banquets. Nowadays they are found in many French recipes, especially along the west coast. Exports from the Languedoc region are flourishing, because the greatest eel lovers live abroad: The Japanese, Scandinavians, and Italians seem to be almost obsessed with them.

Eel is considered a fatty fish, but it is very high in vitamins A and D, and is an excellent source of protein.

This hearty fish ragout is often prepared with red wine and herbs.

Obtain an eel that has been skinned, cleaned and gutted. Cut the eel into 2 in/5 cm chunks.

Plunge the eel chunks in boiling, salted water for 1 minute to remove the fat. Refresh them immediately in cold water. Drain the eel chunks and put to one side. Peel and chop very finely the onions and shallots. Skin the tomatoes and chop the flesh. Peel and crush the garlic.

Heat 1 tbsp olive oil in a pan. Sweat the shallot, onion, garlic, and chopped tomato for 6 minutes until very soft and well combined.

# à la Palavasienne

Dust the eel chunks with flour. Put them in the tomato sauce. Season to taste with salt, pepper, and cayenne pepper. Simmer the eel for 8–10 minutes.

Add the white wine and simmer until reduced by one third. Add the fish stock and boil for 5 minutes. While the stock is boiling, cut the bread into triangles and fry them in the butter. Wash the herbs and chop them finely.

Add the remaining olive oil to the sauce. Add the chopped herbs to the sauce at the last moment. Check the sauce seasoning and adjust as necessary. Serve the eel chunks with the tomato sauce. Garnish with the croutons.

# Monkfish on

| Preparation time: | 30 minutes |
|---|---|
| Time to preserve the garlic: | 35 minutes |
| Cooking time: | 45 minutes |
| Difficulty: | ★ |

**Serves 4**

| 3½ lb/1.5 kg | monkfish |
|---|---|
| 2 tbsp | olive oil |
| | salt |
| | pepper |

**For the eggplant purée:**

| 3½ lb/1.5 kg | eggplant |
|---|---|
| 5 tbsp | olive oil |

| ⅓ cup/20 g | pine kernels |
|---|---|
| | salt |
| | pepper |

**For the bell pepper sauce:**

| 1 | shallot |
|---|---|
| 1 tbsp | olive oil |
| 1 lb/500 g | red bell peppers |
| 8 oz/250 g | tomatoes |
| 1 tbsp | tomato paste |
| 1 clove | garlic |
| 2 cups/ 500 ml | fish stock |
| 4–5/5 g | star anise |
| | salt, pepper |

**For the garnish:**

| 4 cloves | garlic |
|---|---|
| 3½ tbsp/50 ml | olive oil |
| 1 sprig | fresh chervil |

Monkfish medallions is one of the most popular dishes in the south of France. Our head chef has refined this recipe in his Monte Carlo restaurant, saying, "Here the firm flesh of monkfish marries with the sun-drenched flavor of red peppers and the soft smoothness of the eggplant purée, accompanied by toasted pine kernels."

In the Mediterranean, monkfish is commonly known as *baudroie*, but is also called *lotte de mer*. Despite its unattractive appearance, it is highly prized – on account of its firm flesh. If you have trouble filleting fish, ask the fishmonger to do it for you when you purchase the fish. Depending on what is available at the time, many French people use little mackerel, known as *lisettes*, instead.

When prepared as a sauce, as it is in this recipe, the red bell pepper develops its full flavor. This fruit, used as a vegetable, is very closely related to the spicy, elongated peppers from which it differs in size and shape. Red peppers are the most difficult to keep. You should buy firm, smooth fruit with a green stalk that is securely attached to the pepper.

The fish blends extremely well with the eggplant purée. Don't use big eggplants because their flesh is often fibrous and there are too many seeds. When you are buying eggplant, ensure that the fruit has a smooth, tight, shiny skin without blemishes. If the flavor of eggplant is too strong for your taste, you could serve puréed zucchini with the fish instead.

*Clean and gut the fish and make a cut in the outer skin with a pair of scissors. Remove the remaining skins. Cut off the ventral and dorsal fins, and the tail in the opposite direction. Cut the fish into 12 medallions.*

*Using a vegetable peeler, peel strips of skin off the eggplant, keeping them for later. Cut the eggplant in half lengthwise and scoop out the seeds. Season the eggplant. Drizzle each half with 2 tbsp olive oil. Place on a baking sheet and bake for 45 minutes at 320 °F/160 °C.*

*To make the eggplant purée, scoop out the cooked flesh. Chop it finely with the pine kernels. Season to taste with salt and pepper and set to one side. Fry the cloves of garlic in olive oil and keep them for the garnish.*

# Bell Pepper Sauce

To make the bell pepper sauce, sauté the finely chopped shallot in the olive oil. Add the diced red peppers and tomatoes, tomato paste, crushed garlic, fish stock, and star anise. Simmer for 15 minutes. Purée with a hand blender and pass through a sieve. Season to taste.

Cut the strips of eggplant skin into diamonds. Fry them in the remaining olive oil. Put them to one side for the garnish.

Season the monkfish medallions. Fry them in olive oil for 3 minutes. Arrange 3 tbsp eggplant purée on a plate, each with a monkfish medallion in the center. Spoon the bell pepper sauce around the fish and eggplant. Garnish with chervil, fried eggplant diamonds, and fried garlic.

# Fillet of Salt Cod

Preparation time: 20 minutes
Fish soaking time: 24 hours
Cooking time: 1 hour
Difficulty: ★★

**Serves 4**

| | |
|---|---|
| 1 lb/500 g | dried, salt cod |
| 1 clove | garlic |
| ⅓ cup + 1½ tbsp/100 ml | light cream |
| 1 pinch | dried thyme |
| ⅞ cup/100 g | flour |
| ⅓ cup + 1½ tbsp/ 100 ml | olive oil |
| 1 | small potato |

oil for frying
salt, pepper

**For the vegetable accompaniment (samfaïne):**

| | |
|---|---|
| 1 | red bell pepper |
| ½ | green bell pepper |
| 1 | eggplant |
| 2 | yellow onions |
| 3 | tomatoes |
| ⅓ cup + 1½ tbsp/ 100 ml | olive oil |
| | salt, pepper |

**For the garnish:**

fresh chervil (optional)

The roots of Catalan cuisine lie to the north and south of the Pyrenees. Culinary influences from cities such as Gerona or Barcelona have persisted in Perpignan for centuries. *Morue en samfaïne* exemplifies the cooking culture that originated in these two regions. The Catalan word *samfaïne* is the term for a slightly caramelized ratatouille. The vegetables are cooked until all the moisture has evaporated. The *samfaïne* is finished when it looks like a purée.

*Morue*, the dried salt cod beloved of Catalans, north through south, must be soaked the day before you need it. Change the water frequently. This cold saltwater fish is only called *morue* when it dried or salted. When fresh, cod is called *cabillaud*.

The types of vegetable in this recipe are representative of the whole Mediterranean region: The dish gets its sweet taste from the bell peppers. This fruit, used as a vegetable,

is closely related to the elongated, hot peppers. Red bell peppers are the most delicate and difficult to store. You should therefore buy firm, smooth fruit with solid green stalks. Another indispensable ingredient is the eggplant. This elongated, slightly rounded fruit, which originated in India, has a smooth, shiny purple skin. Onions and tomatoes are also traditional ratatouille ingredients.

To finish off the dish, Jean-Claude Vila prepares a garlic sauce. Garlic originated in Central Asia and is known for its powerful flavor. If you use garlic, remove the core from the cloves and blanch the cloves in boiling water about three times.

*Prepare the vegetables for the samfaïne. Cut the bell peppers into strips, dice the eggplant, and peel and chop the onions.*

*Fry them all in olive oil for 10 minutes. Add 4 tbsp water, salt and pepper, cover, and braise for 30 minutes.*

*Put the tomatoes in a bowl. Pour boiling water over and leave them for a few minutes. Drain the tomatoes, skin and deseed them. Dice the tomatoes and add them to the vegetables. Simmer for 5–6 minutes.*

# with Samfaïne

For the garlic sauce, peel the garlic and remove the cores. Blanch the garlic in boiling water, repeating the process three times. Stir in the cream. At the last minute add the dried thyme. Season with salt and pepper.

Drain the soaked fish and cut it into 4 pieces. Toss the fish in the flour and fry in olive oil for 1 minute on each side. Pile the samfaïne on top of the fish and bake in the oven for 7 minutes at a temperature of 350 °F/180 °C.

Peel the potato and slice it thinly. Wash and dry the slices, and fry them in hot oil until golden brown. Drain the potato chips and season with salt. Arrange the potato chips on a plate with the baked fish. Spoon a semicircle of sauce onto the plate. Garnish with chervil.

# Monkfish in

Preparation time: 15 minutes
Cooking time: 10 minutes
Difficulty: ✶

**Serves 4**

| | |
|---|---|
| 1½ lb/800 g | monkfish |
| 1 | onion |
| 3 cloves | garlic |
| 2 tbsp | olive oil |
| 12 | potatoes |

| | |
|---|---|
| ¾ cup/200 ml | light cream |
| 5 | egg yolks |
| 8 oz/250 g | packet puff pastry |
| | salt |
| | pepper |

**For the garlic mayonnaise (aioli):**

| | |
|---|---|
| 5 cloves | garlic |
| 4 | egg yolks |
| ¾ cup/200 ml | olive oil |
| | salt |

This fish dish, *bourride*, is typically Provençal. It tastes best in Marseilles, especially in the "Miramar" restaurant, where our chef is based, but it is available in other cities throughout the south of France.

The fish in this recipe, the famous monkfish, has a disproportionately large head and a flat body. Its massive mouth is armed with terrifying teeth – after all, the monkfish is a carnivore that can grow up to 6 ½ feet/2 meters long!

If you can get this saltwater fish, ensure that the flesh is gleaming white and pink around the bones. The best time of year for monkfish is spring. It is very popular, not just because of its flavor, but also because it's easy to prepare and does not fall apart during cooking.

Monkfish flesh is so firm it is reminiscent of red meat. In fact, sometimes it is prepared like a leg of lamb, spiked with garlic, for instance. If you use it for another recipe, don't use too much liquid, because monkfish itself gives off a lot of liquor during cooking.

To make the fish stock in our recipe, buy some fish bones and trimmings. To vary the taste, you could follow Jean-Claude Minguella's advice and try the recipe with different white fish such as whiting, porgy, cod, John Dory, or sea bass.

If the garlic mayonnaise separates, transfer it to a blender, and add an ice cube whilst blending. When serving the dish, scatter a little chopped parsley over the potatoes.

*Clean and gut the fish, remove the skin. Fish stock: Peel the onion and garlic. Fry them in 2 tbsp olive oil and add the fish trimmings (see above). Pour 10 cups/2½ l water into the pan. Simmer for 20 minutes. Reduce. Strain through a sieve and reserve 8 cups/2 l stock.*

*Cut the fish into 4 pieces and poach in 4 cups/1 l fish stock for 8–10 minutes. Take the monkfish out and keep it warm. Put the fish stock to one side. Peel the potatoes and boil them in the other 4 cups/1 l fish stock. Drain.*

*To make the aioli, peel 5 cloves of garlic and remove the cores. Chop the garlic and add the egg yolks. Season with salt. Beat the olive oil into the egg mixture, a few drops at a time. Remove one third of the mayonnaise and put aside.*

# Garlic Cream

Heat the fish stock in which the monkfish was cooked. Season it to taste with salt and pepper and strain it through a sieve. Return it to the pan, add the cream, and simmer for 2–3 minutes. Keep the sauce warm.

Beat 4 egg yolks into the main portion of mayonnaise. Beat this mixture into the hot fish sauce and stir well. The sauce should be quite thick. Heat the sauce on low heat, stirring all the time, then strain through a fine sieve, and keep it warm in a double boiler.

Cut crescents from the puff pastry. Brush with the remaining egg yolk and bake at 430 °F/220 °C for 8 minutes. Arrange on plates the monkfish, potatoes, crescents, and some reserved aioli on toasted bread. Pour half the sauce into the plates. Serve the other half separately.

# Pot-au-feu

*Preparation time:* 30 minutes
*Soaking the*
*    marrow bones:* 24 hours
*Cooking time:* 35 minutes
*Difficulty:* ★

**Serves 4**

**For the vegetables:**

| | |
|---|---|
| 2 | carrots |
| 2 | baby turnips or kohlrabi |
| 2 sticks | celery |
| 1 | potato |
| 4 | baby onions |

| | |
|---|---|
| ¾ cup/200 ml | fish stock |
| 1 lb/500 g | green asparagus |

| | |
|---|---|
| 4 pieces | sea bass, each 5 oz/150 g |
| 4 pieces | marrow bone, 1 in/3 cm in diameter |
| 4 tsp | truffle juice |
| 1 | bay leaf |
| 1 | small truffle |
| 1 | potato |
| | oil for frying |
| | rock salt |
| 1 tsp | olive oil |
| | salt, pepper |

**For the garnish:**

| | |
|---|---|
| | celery leaves (optional) |

A *pot-au-feu* is very specifically French. What was once a farmer's stew consists of broth, meat, and vegetables. Although there are countless recipes for this dish, our chef has had an idea for an innovative version, replacing the meat with fish.

Mediterranean sea bass is a member of the serranid family. This is a fish that is very popular in the region. Ask your fishmonger for wild sea bass, which has a much better flavor than the farmed fish. If you can't find sea bass, you could always use porgy instead.

The use of truffles gives this dish an added attraction. These highly coveted and expensive fungi were known in ancient times. The Ancient Egyptians liked them best surrounded in goose fat and baked, and the Greeks and Romans ascribed extraordinary aphrodisiacal powers to them.

The fungus itself is an irregular, rounded lump. It's usually black or dark brown, sometimes gray, or white.

When you buy the vegetables ensure that you buy large specimens. After cooking the vegetables, refresh them in ice water so they retain their attractive green color. Marrowbone is often used in *pot-au-feu*. It must be soaked for 24 hours in cold water, changing the water frequently.

When serving, first arrange the vegetables on the plate and then put the fish on them. The broth is poured over the top. You could also drizzle a few drops of olive oil over the dish if you like.

*Wash and peel the vegetables. Leave a small piece of stalk on the carrots and turnips. Cut the celery into pieces and carefully remove any stringy bits.*

*Put the fish stock in a pan and add 3 cups/750 ml water. Season with salt and pepper. Add the vegetables. As soon as they are cooked, remove them, and set them aside. Cook the asparagus separately in salted water for 10 minutes.*

*Cook the pieces of fish and marrowbone in the vegetable liquor for 7–8 minutes. Add the truffle juice, the bay leaf, and half the truffle cut into small dice.*

# with Sea Bass

Heat the vegetables in the broth and add the other half of the truffle, sliced.

Wash the potato, do not peel it. Cut it into wedges lengthwise. Blanch the potato in boiling, salted water, then refresh it in cold water for 2 minutes. Pat the wedges dry, then fry them.

Drain the potato wedges on kitchen paper and dredge them in the rock salt while still warm. Arrange the drained vegetables on the plate, then the drained fish and marrowbone. Pour over the broth. Drizzle a little olive oil over the dish, and garnish with celery leaves, if using.

# Red Mullet with

Preparation time: 1 hour 20 minutes
Cooking time: 15 minutes
Difficulty: ★

**Serves 4**

| | |
|---|---|
| 4 | red mullet, each 5 oz/150 g |
| 10 cloves | garlic |
| 4 tsp/20 g | cornstarch |
| ⅜ stick/40 g | butter |
| 3 oz/80 g | fresh peas (shucked) |
| 2 tbsp | olive oil |
| 2 | tomatoes |
| 1 stick | celery |
| 1 | lemon |
| 8 | black olives |

| | |
|---|---|
| 3 | basil leaves |
| ¾ cup/200 ml | whipping cream |
| | salt, pepper |

**For the sauce vierge:**

| | |
|---|---|
| 1 tbsp | olive oil |
| 1 tsp | aged wine vinegar |
| 1 dash | Tabasco sauce |
| | salt, pepper |

**For the garnish:**

| | |
|---|---|
| 4 slivers | parmesan |
| 8 | basil leaves |
| | celery leaves |
| | rock salt |

In the Mediterranean, red mullet has been prized since ancient times. If you cannot get hold of red mullet, use red snapper instead. Like red mullet, it is rich in proteins, iodine, iron, and phosphorus. It is imperative that you stick to the specified cooking time as it will lose its flavor if overcooked. Depending on what is available, you can also use porgy or John Dory instead of red mullet. Even if you buy the fish ready filleted, remember that you will need to remove the tiny bones with a pair of tweezers.

Garlic plays an important role in this fish dish. Garlic bulbs originate from Central Asia, are a member of the lily family, and are known for their medicinal properties. The powerful taste becomes milder if you blanch the garlic. After peeling, plunge the garlic into boiling water, then into cold water, repeating the process three times.

When preparing this dish you need clarified butter. To

make clarified butter, slowly heat the butter and skim off the whey that rises to the surface as a white foam. The garlic won't burn in the clarified butter. The garlic can also be seasoned with celery salt. When scaling the red mullet, work from the tail towards the head.

*Sauce vierge* is a cold marinade that is typical of the south of France. The tomatoes must be peeled and deseeded. This dressing is just warmed a little, not heated. The separate cream sauce will be lighter if you whip and fold in a tablespoon of cream, before stirring in the rest. Depending on the time of year, baby fava beans are a welcome addition to *sauce vierge*.

Scale the red mullet, gut them, and wash them. Using a knife, fillet the fish, and remove the bones using a pair of tweezers.

Cut the peeled garlic into thin slices and blanch them. Then carefully coat the blanched garlic in cornstarch, and layer it like scales on the skin side of the fish. Drizzle clarified butter over the garlic.

Boil the peas in salted water for 8 minutes. Marinate them in olive oil with the skinned, deseeded and diced tomatoes, chopped celery, peeled lemon, olives, and chopped basil. Season with salt and pepper, and add the ingredients for the sauce vierge. Heat half of the mixture.

# Sauce Vierge

Purée the other half of the mixture with a hand blender and stir in the cream. Simmer gently for 5 minutes, and season to taste with salt and pepper.

Fry the red mullet fillets in olive oil first on the skin side, then on the flesh side, for 2 minutes each side.

Spoon the sauce vierge into the middle of a plate and arrange a red mullet fillet on top. Surround it with a pool of cream sauce. Finally garnish with parmesan slivers, basil and celery leaves, as well as rock salt.

# Scallops with

| | |
|---|---|
| Preparation time: | 1 hour |
| Soaking the | |
| scallops: | 45 minutes |
| Cooking time: | 5 minutes |
| Difficulty: | ★ |

**Serves 4**

| | |
|---|---|
| 12 | medium scallops |
| 5 oz/150 g | mesclun |
| | rock salt |

**For the stuffing:**

| | |
|---|---|
| 2 cloves | garlic |
| 1 bunch | fresh flat-leaf parsley |
| ½ | fresh chile |

| | |
|---|---|
| 1 | large shallot |
| 1 | scallion |
| 1 stick/100 g | butter |
| 2 slices | white bread |
| 2 tbsp | olive oil |
| | juice of ½ lemon |
| | salt |

**For the balsamic vinaigrette:**

| | |
|---|---|
| 3 tbsp | olive oil |
| 1 tbsp | balsamic vinegar |
| | salt |
| | pepper |

**For the garnish:**

| | |
|---|---|
| | rock salt |

What is original about this recipe is the way in which the scallops are prepared. Our chef cooks the meat in the shell. No great culinary skills are required for this dish and yet, because of its ingredients, it is representative of the delicious ingredients from the south of France.

Scallops, *coquilles Saint-Jacques* in French, are a large mussel that lives on the floor of the Atlantic Ocean and the Mediterranean Sea, and which moves by opening and closing. It's flat on one side and corrugated on the other. The ridged shell measures 4–6 inches/10–15 centimeters across. You should only buy scallops that are tightly closed. Ask your fishmonger to prepare the scallops without cutting through the muscle. Don't forget to soak them at home. The rock salt is used to support the scallops so that they don't tip over.

The firm, white flesh of this shellfish, which is very popular in France, has a delicate flavor. Scallop fishing is regulated in Europe, and usually takes place between the end of September and beginning of May. In the past, a scallop-shell badge was a sign that a pilgrim had made the journey to the shrine at Santiago de Compostela, in Spain.

The savory stuffing is an important component of this dish and gives the scallops a slightly acidic flavor. Depending on what is available, our chef says you can also enrich the stuffing with black olives, diced lemon, or capers.

Mesclun consists of baby salad leaves from the south of France. These include winter frisée, radicchio, Belgian endive, corn salad, dandelion, chervil, oak leaf lettuce, and purslane. You can buy ready mixed bags of mesclun.

*Open the scallops. Run a knife blade along between the shells without cutting through the muscle. Remove the flat side of the shell.*

*Clean the scallops by gripping beneath the dark pouch and pulling out the membrane and beard. The meat should stay attached to the shell. Soak the scallops for 45 minutes to rinse out sand and other contaminants.*

*To make the stuffing, chop the garlic, parsley, chile, shallot, and scallion very finely. Dice the butter and bread.*

# Mixed Salad Leaves

Mix together the diced bread and butter. Add the other stuffing ingredients and the olive oil. Add the lemon juice and stir well to combine.

Season the scallop meat with salt, and gently lift it with a spoon without completely dislodging it. Fill each scallop shell with 1 tbsp stuffing and place the shell on a baking sheet filled with rock salt. Bake the scallops in the oven for 5 minutes at 465 °F/250 °C.

Rinse the mixed salad leaves. Beat together the vinaigrette ingredients. Place a scallop shell on a bed of rock salt and serve accompanied by the mixed salad.

# Red Mullet

Preparation time: 40 minutes
Cooking time: 40 minutes
Difficulty: ★★

**Serves 4**

| | |
|---|---|
| 1 lb/500 g | baby squid |
| 3 tbsp | olive oil |
| 6 | red mullet, each 5 oz/150 g |
| | salt |
| | pepper |

**For the broiled vegetables (escalivada):**

| | |
|---|---|
| 2 | tomatoes |
| 1 | eggplant |

| | |
|---|---|
| 1 | red bell pepper |
| 6 cloves | garlic |
| 4 | scallions |
| 4 tbsp | olive oil |
| | salt |
| | pepper |

**For the sea urchin sauce:**

| | |
|---|---|
| 12 | sea urchins |
| 3 cloves | garlic |
| 2 tsp | fish stock |
| 4 tbsp | olive oil |

Land and sea meet in this dish where Jean Plouzennec serves the fish as a kebab.

*Escalivada* is a mixture of broiled or roasted vegetables, bell peppers, tomatoes, eggplant, onions, and garlic. You'll have no problem in finding different types of vegetable, because they are available all year round.

When you take the bell pepper out of the oven, wrap it in aluminum foil. It continues cooking and the skin comes away very easily. It's simple to make soft eggplant flesh into dumplings. Dampen a teaspoon, scoop up a little eggplant purée, and shape it carefully with a second teaspoon.

Make sure the red mullet (or, if unavailable, red snapper) that you buy are good quality. Even if you buy filleted fish, you should make sure every last bone is removed by using a pair of tweezers. You should always cook the fillets on the skin side first, and then for a little longer on the flesh side. If you can't get red mullet or red snapper, use monkfish, which withstands cooking at high temperatures very well.

There is very little difference between baby squid and very small cuttlefish. The name depends on the time of year and the region. if you can't find baby squid, you can use white squid meat instead.

You can prepare this recipe without the sea urchin sauce. Sea urchins are a seafood that is rarely available. Only passionate gourmets believe they are indispensable. Wear thick gloves when opening the sea urchins because the soft flesh around the mouth is surrounded by razor-sharp spines. Their delicate flavor is a perfect complement to the kebab.

*Preheat the oven to 400 °F/200 °C. Deseed and quarter the tomatoes. Bake the eggplant for 30–40 minutes, bell pepper for 30 minutes, unpeeled garlic for 15–20 minutes and scallions for 10 minutes. Scoop out the eggplant flesh. Purée with 2 garlic cloves. Set vegetables aside.*

*Dry the tomatoes for 5 minutes in the oven at 210 °F/100 °C. Season with salt and pepper. Drizzle 3 tbsp olive oil over all the vegetables.*

*Clean and prepare the baby squid and pat dry. Heat 2 tbsp olive oil in a skillet and fry the squid in it. Fillet the red mullet and cut the fillets into even-sized pieces. Remove all the bones. Add seasoning.*

# and Squid

Slide pieces of red mullet and squid alternately onto wooden skewers. Sauté them for 2–3 minutes on each side in 1 tbsp olive oil.

Stir the remaining olive oil into the garlic and eggplant purée. Arrange a scoop of purée on each plate. Arrange the baked and peeled garlic and the baked vegetables on the plate.

Sea urchin sauce: In a warmed pan combine 3 roasted and puréed cloves of garlic with the sea urchin meat. Add the hot fish stock, then add the olive oil and beat the mixture like a mayonnaise. Drizzle the sea urchin sauce around the plates with the fish skewers.

# Meat & Poultry

# Lamb with

Preparation time: 40 minutes
Cooking time: 30 minutes
Difficulty: ★

**Serves 4**

3½ lb/1.5 kg    saddle of lamb
4 tbsp    olive oil
generous ¾ cup/
200 ml    white wine
2½ tbsp/40 ml    veal stock

1 sprig    fresh rosemary
2¼ lb/1 kg    salsify, preferably
      scorzonera
scant ⅛ cup/
20 g    superfine sugar
      salt
      pepper

**For the garnish:**
4 stems    redcurrants
4 sprigs    fresh rosemary

Black salsify is the traditional ingredient for this recipe. In summer, in Pardailhan, a little village of 160 souls in the Hérault, the locals laugh at the tourists' astonishment that it exists. It's the same as the plant that is cultivated for its fleshy root, elongated or rounded, from pale yellow to white, with leaves that are often purple at the base. In Pardailhan, however, the salsify has a hard, black, but still tender skin. There have been several attempts to grow it in other areas. The plants may have been black, but they did not taste like the originals. The caramel-like flavor of Pardailhan scorzonera makes it unique.

Those who don't live near Pardailhan need not bother to look for scorzonera, because production and sales are purely local. But you can still make the recipe with the usual types of salsify, or our chef suggests celeriac purée as an alternative accompaniment.

The time allowed to cook the lamb fillets is important; otherwise these tender, juicy cuts dry out. Like fillet of veal, which can be used in this recipe as an alternative, the lamb is cooked pink.

Rosemary is a Mediterranean herb and is a member of the labiate family. When cooked with the lamb it gives it a strong flavor. You could also use fresh or dried tarragon. This herb is also typical of the scent of the *garrigue*, the name given to Provençal scrubland.

The redcurrants add a splash of color to the plate. If you prefer raspberries, they can be used instead for a garnish, as can a cherry tomato.

*Bone the saddle of lamb. Cut out the backbone and remove the fillets. Cut away any fat and skin. Reserve the bones and refrigerate the meat.*

*To make the lamb gravy, sauté the bones in 1 tbsp olive oil. Deglaze the pan with the white wine. Add the veal stock and 1 cup/250 ml water. Add the rosemary and cook it with the gravy for 10 minutes.*

*Wash the scorzonera, peel it, and cut it into cylindrical batons. Boil the scorzonera in salted water for 10 minutes, then drain it.*

# Scorzonera

Brown the scorzonera in a pan in 2 tbsp olive oil for 5 minutes. Sprinkle the sugar over it and leave it to caramelize.

Fry the lamb fillets in the remaining olive oil until golden brown. Season with salt and pepper, then transfer them to the oven, and roast them until the meat is cooked.

Leave the fillets to rest for 5 minutes, then slice them. Arrange the slices on a plate and pour some of the strained gravy over them. Arrange the pieces of scorzonera around the lamb, and garnish with redcurrants and rosemary.

# Lamb Stuffed

Preparation time: 40 minutes
Chilling time: 1 hour
Cooking time: 1 hour 20 minutes
Difficulty: ★★★

**Serves 4**

| | |
|---|---|
| 1 saddle | lamb |
| 3 tbsp | olive oil |
| 1 lb/500 g | phyllo (filo) pastry |
| 4 cloves | garlic |
| | salt |
| | pepper |

**For the tomatoes Provençal:**

| | |
|---|---|
| 2 | tomatoes |
| 5 slices | white bread |
| 3 cloves | garlic |
| ¼ bunch | fresh parsley |

**For the spinach filling:**

| | |
|---|---|
| 10 oz/300 g | spinach |
| 10 oz/300 g | Swiss chard |
| 1 tbsp | olive oil |
| 3 sprigs | fresh thyme |
| 1 clove | garlic |
| | salt |

**For the garlic cream sauce:**

| | |
|---|---|
| 8 cloves | garlic |
| 1¼ cups/300 g | whipping cream |
| 1¼ cups/300 ml | milk |

**For the zucchini towers:**

| | |
|---|---|
| 2 each | zucchini, potatoes |
| 1 | soft goat milk cheese |
| 3½ tbsp/50 ml | light cream |

**For the lamb gravy:**

| | |
|---|---|
| | lamb bones |
| 2 cloves | garlic |
| 3 sprigs | fresh thyme |
| 1 | leek |
| 2 | tomatoes |
| | salt, pepper |

**For the garnish:**

| | |
|---|---|
| few sprigs | fresh thyme |

Because he retains close ties to his home region of the Bouches-du-Rhône, Francis Robin presents this lamb stuffed with spinach. He prepares it using the very tasty meat from the merino sheep around Arles. These sheep grow up outdoors and graze the meadows in summer. In the past, this breed of sheep was only kept for wool, but now merino lamb is used in a variety of dishes.

The saddle of lamb, which our chef has chosen for his recipe, comes from the area above the haunches, at the base of the animal's back, and is extremely tender. You could also use shoulder of lamb, which should be boned carefully. Save the bones because they will be chopped and used for the gravy.

In this recipe, only the green part of the Swiss chard is used. The ribs can be used in another recipe. Buy Swiss chard with small leaves. After blanching the spinach in boiling water, put it in cold water to refresh it. In this way it will retain its attractive, green color.

Try to buy baby zucchini. They should be firm and evenly colored. They will keep for up to a week in your refrigerator's salad compartment.

Here, Francis Robin uses a soft goat milk cheese with a refreshing, acidic note. Blanch a dozen cloves of garlic to contribute to the success of this recipe. The remainder can be used as a garnish.

*Bone the saddle of lamb and remove as much fat as possible. Chop the bones into small pieces and keep them for the gravy. Remove the fillets and brush them with 1 tbsp olive oil. Season with salt and pepper. Brown the fillets in a skillet, let them cool, then refrigerate them.*

*To make the spinach filling, blanch the spinach and Swiss chard in boiling salted water. Refresh them in ice water. Then squeeze out all the liquid and chop the leaves coarsely. Combine the leaves with 1 tbsp olive oil. Season with chopped thyme, chopped garlic, and salt.*

*Lamb gravy: Fry the chopped lamb bones with the chopped garlic, thyme, green part of the leek, and tomatoes. Add 4 cups/1 l water, and boil until reduced by three quarters. Season and strain through a sieve. Spread the spinach/Swiss chard mixture over the lamb fillets.*

# with Spinach

Brush sheets of phyllo pastry with oil. Place the lamb fillets on top and wrap. Brown the pastry parcels in a skillet, transfer to the oven and roast at 400 °F/200 °C for 10 minutes. Blanch 8 cloves garlic 3 times. Put in a bowl. Add the cream and milk. Purée, then sieve.

Blanch the halved zucchini in boiling water, then scoop out the seeds. Boil the potatoes in salted water and mash. Add 2 tbsp garlic cream sauce, the goat milk cheese, and the cream. Season with salt, then beat all the ingredients together to a smooth consistency, use it to fill the zucchini.

Mince the bread to make breadcrumbs. Combine with the chopped garlic and parsley. Halve the tomatoes and scoop out. Fill the tomatoes with the breadcrumb mixture. Top each tomato half with an unpeeled clove of garlic and bake in the oven for 8–10 minutes at 400 °F/200 °C.

# Fillet of Lamb

| Preparation time: | 1 hour 15 minutes |
|---|---|
| Cooking time: | 1 hour 30 minutes |
| Difficulty: | ★★ |

**Serves 4**

| 3½ lb/1.5 kg | saddle of lamb |
|---|---|
| 1 tbsp | olive oil |
| | salt, pepper |

**For the layered vegetables:**

| 1 | zucchini |
|---|---|
| 1 | eggplant |
| 1 | onion |
| 2 | tomatoes |
| ½ bulb | garlic |

| 2 sprigs | fresh thyme |
|---|---|
| | olive oil |

**For the lamb gravy:**

| 1 | carrot |
|---|---|
| 1 | stalk celery |
| 1 | onion |
| 1 sprig | fresh thyme |
| 1 sprig | fresh parsley |
| ½ bulb | garlic |
| 1 | bay leaf |
| 1 tbsp | olive oil |

**For the garnish:**

| 8 | basil leaves |
|---|---|
| | oil for frying |

All the ingredients in this recipe make it a classic of French cuisine. Saddle of lamb comes from the animal's rump, above the haunches, and is extremely tender and juicy. If you have trouble filleting the meat, ask your butcher to prepare it for you. Our chef advises that you keep to the cooking time as closely as possible; the fillets, which dry out easily, are roasted pink. The layered Provençal vegetables are also a good accompaniment to guinea fowl or pigeon.

When preparing the lamb gravy, don't chop the garlic. Only add the salt halfway through the cooking time.

This dish combines all the flavors of Provence, this time incorporating braised onion. Ensure that the onion is translucent before you add the water.

Zucchini are elongated and evenly colored, varying from light to dark depending on the variety. The cut mark on the stalk should be fresh and white. Wash the zucchini under running water and dry them before you slice them.

Our chef always sautés the zucchini before the eggplant, because the latter soaks up so much oil. The elongated or round eggplant originates from India and first reached France in the 17th century. The smooth, shiny skin encases pale, firm flesh. To prevent the eggplant soaking up too much oil, take it out of the pan immediately after frying and drain it on absorbent kitchen paper. Only then should it be seasoned.

The basil leaves are fried in hot oil for a couple of seconds. As basil epitomizes the south, it is ideal.

*Using a sharp knife, take the lamb fillets off the bone. Start on the top side of the saddle and cut along the bones with the point of the knife. Separate the belly flaps and remove the fat. Reserve the belly flaps and bones for the lamb gravy.*

*Carefully trim the fillets and remove all the fat. Then make the lamb gravy.*

*Fry the lamb bones and belly for 10 minutes. Add the diced carrot, celery, chopped onion, chopped thyme and parsley, and whole cloves of garlic. Sweat for 15 minutes. Cover with water, add the bay leaf, and simmer for 1½ hours. Strain, season to taste. Simmer for 5 minutes.*

# in a Garlic Jus

Fry the sliced zucchini and eggplant in olive oil. Sweat the sliced onion in 1 tbsp olive oil for 15 minutes, season, and add water. Slice the tomatoes and season with salt and pepper. Sweat the tomatoes with grated garlic, chopped thyme, and 1 tbsp olive oil for 10 minutes.

Using a circular cookie cutter or ring mold, layer sliced eggplant, braised onions, sliced zucchini, and finally tomatoes. Bake in the oven for 5 minutes immediately before you want to serve them.

Season the lamb fillets with salt and pepper. Fry them in 1 tbsp olive oil for 10 minutes, to seal them. Slice the fillets. Arrange them on the plate with the layered vegetable stacks. Garnish with deep-fried basil, and lamb gravy to which a little chopped garlic has been added.

# Loin of Lamb

Preparation time: 45 minutes
Cooking time: 1 hour 15 minutes
Difficulty: ★

**Serves 4**

| | |
|---|---|
| 2 | white onions |
| 2 tbsp | olive oil |
| 1 sprig | fresh thyme |
| 1 | bay leaf |
| 2 | loins of lamb, each 1½ lb/700 g |
| 1 | zucchini |
| 1 | eggplant |
| 3 | beefsteak tomatoes, each 2 ½ oz/60 g |
| | salt, pepper |

**For the herb crust:**

| | |
|---|---|
| 1 bunch | fresh chives |
| 1 bunch | fresh chervil |
| 1 bunch | fresh tarragon |
| 2 | egg yolks |
| 7 oz/200 g | prepared mustard |

**For the lamb gravy:**

| | |
|---|---|
| 1 | carrot |
| 1 | onion |
| 1 sprig | fresh parsley |
| 3½ tbsp/50 ml | white wine |
| 1 tbsp | olive oil |

**For the garlic oil:**

| | |
|---|---|
| 4 cloves | garlic |
| 1 sprig | fresh thyme |
| 1 | bay leaf |
| ⅔ cup/150 ml | olive oil |

**For the garnish:**

| | |
|---|---|
| 4 sprigs | rosemary, 1 clove garlic |

With this recipe Joël Garault, chef at the restaurant in the "Hermitage" hotel, Monte Carlo, pays homage to the Principality and its famous cliffs.

Loin of lamb with a herb crust is a traditional dish from the Provençal countryside. It's a very popular cut of lamb. According to our chef, each piece, when trimmed, should weigh 1½ pounds/700 grams. If you can't obtain lamb you could serve veal or poultry with the vegetable rosettes.

Spicy mustard plays an important role in the golden herb crust. The seeds of the mustard plant, indigenous to the Mediterranean region, are used to make the yellow condiment of the same name that can be mild or hot. The mustard combines with the flavor of the lamb to produce a characteristic taste.

Of course herbs are also part of the herb crust. Sometimes our chef uses basil instead of tarragon, or flat-leaf parsley instead of chervil. The slightly peppery flavor of chives is, on the other hand, an essential component. Fresh chives are available from spring to fall. They should not be in flower and the blades should be slender and dark green.

To save time you can prepare the vegetable rosettes a day before you need them. They will be nice and juicy when reheated. Choose zucchini, eggplant, and tomatoes that are roughly the same size. Reserve the olive oil in which you fry the unpeeled garlic, because the vegetable rosettes are coated in it too.

Loin of lamb with a herb crust is very simple. The only garnish required is garlic and rosemary.

Peel and chop the onions and sweat them in olive oil for 10 minutes on low heat. Season with salt and pepper. Add the chopped thyme and the bay leaf.

Remove the back bones, belly flaps and fat from the lamb. Separate the lower part to a depth of 2 fingers wide, and free the ribs. Keep the scraps. To make the garlic oil, sweat the garlic, thyme, and bay leaf in olive oil on low heat for 35 minutes. Drain and keep the oil.

Slice the vegetables. Soak in the cooled garlic oil. Place round ring molds on a baking sheet. Divide the onions between the ring molds, then layer the sliced vegetables on top in a rosette shape. Season, drizzle over a little olive oil. Bake at 320 °F/160 °C for 20 minutes.

# with a Herb Crust

To make the herb crust, finely chop the chives, chervil, and tarragon. In a bowl, combine them with the egg yolks and mustard.

Season the loins of lamb and scraps. Bake in the oven at 400 °F/200 °C, together with the chopped gravy ingredients, except for the wine, for 20 minutes. Deglaze the pan with the white wine. Spread the herb paste over the loins and roast at 465 °F/250 °C for 3 minutes.

Strain the gravy and season to taste with salt and pepper. Leave the loins of lamb to rest for 5 minutes. Then cut them into chops. Arrange 3 chops and a vegetable rosette on each plate. Garnish with rosemary, a halved clove of garlic, and a spoonful of gravy.

# Stuffed

*Preparation time:*    1 hour
*Cooking time:*    2 hours 40 minutes
*Difficulty:*    ★★★

**Serves 4**

**For the stuffed rabbit thighs:**
| | |
|---|---|
| 4 | young rabbit thighs |
| 1 | pig's caul |
| 2 cloves | garlic |
| 4 | zucchini |
| 4 cups/1 l | olive oil |
| | salt |
| | pepper |

**For the rabbit gravy:**
| | |
|---|---|
| | rabbit bones |
| 1 tbsp | olive oil |
| 1 | onion |
| 1 clove | garlic |

| | |
|---|---|
| 3 sprigs | fresh parsley |
| 2 sprigs | fresh thyme |
| ⅛ stick/20 g | butter |

**For the caramelized onions:**
| | |
|---|---|
| 3 | medium onions |
| 2 sprigs | fresh thyme |

| | |
|---|---|
| 2 tbsp | olive oil |
| | salt, pepper |

**For the garlic cream sauce:**
| | |
|---|---|
| 1 bulb | garlic |
| ⅞ cup/200 ml | milk |
| 1¼ cups/300 ml | cream |
| | salt, pepper |

**For the garbanzo flour batons:**
| | |
|---|---|
| 1 cup/200 g | garbanzo bean flour |
| 3 tbsp | olive oil |
| | olive oil for frying |
| | salt |

**For the braised tomatoes (optional):**
| | |
|---|---|
| 1 | onion |
| 2 cloves | garlic |
| 2 sprigs | fresh thyme |
| 4 | small tomatoes |
| ¾ cup/200 ml | chicken stock |
| | olive oil |

In rural southern France, rabbit is often on the menu. The little rodents, found everywhere, are normally farmed. Wild rabbits only appear at the butcher's during the game hunting season. Check for top-quality meat that is firm, but not too fatty, and is a deep pink color.

This creation by Francis Robin demands a certain know-how. The rabbit thighs must be prepared carefully. The temperature of the olive oil is also very important. It's best to use a meat thermometer, because the temperature of 160 degrees Fahrenheit/70 degrees Celsius must be accurate for a guaranteed result. Before serving, the stuffed rabbit thighs should be broiled briefly to cook off any unnecessary fat.

Garlic is another popular ingredient. Ensure you select very firm bulbs, preferably of pink garlic, and store it in the driest place in your kitchen. When preparing it, you should remove the core from each clove, because that way it is easier to digest.

This celebration dish not only takes on a colorful note, but an acidic one, when served with braised tomatoes. To make them, sauté chopped onion, crushed garlic, and two sprigs of thyme in olive oil. Then add skinned, deseeded and diced tomatoes. Add the chicken stock and simmer until reduced. Arrange the tomatoes on a plate as an accompaniment, next to the fried garbanzo flour batons. The dish should be served piping hot.

*To make the caramelized onions, peel and finely chop the onions. Sweat the onions with the chopped thyme in 2 tbsp olive oil. Season with salt and pepper, and leave to sweat down for 5–10 minutes. Let the onion mixture cool, then refrigerate it.*

*Bone the rabbit thighs to create a pocket. Season the inside with salt and pepper. Reserve all the bones. Stuff the thighs with the caramelized onions, wrap them in the pig's caul, and place them in little ring molds.*

*Heat the olive oil to 160 °F/80 °C in a large saucepan. Add 2 unpeeled cloves of garlic. Fry the rabbit thighs in hot oil at 160 °F/70 °C for one hour. Score grooves down the length of the zucchini, then slice them. Blanch them in boiling, salted water, and put them to one side.*

# Rabbit Thighs

To make the rabbit gravy, chop the bones and sauté them in 1 tbsp olive oil with chopped onion, garlic, parsley, and thyme. Add 4 cups/1 l water. Simmer on low heat for 1 hour, stir frequently. Boil the broth until reduced, then strain it and beat in a generous ⅛ stick/20 g butter.

Beat together the garbanzo bean flour, 1 cup/250 ml cold water, and 1 tbsp olive oil. Gradually add the garbanzo batter to 3 cups/750 ml boiling salted water, with the remaining olive oil. Leave the resulting dough to cool. Cut into batons and deep fry them in olive oil.

For the garlic cream sauce, peel the garlic and remove the cores. Blanch three times, then drain. Simmer for 25 minutes in the milk and cream. Season, purée, and sieve. Arrange the rabbit along with the garbanzo batons on a bed of zucchini. Drizzle gravy and sauce onto the plate.

# Provençal

Preparation time: 15 minutes
Marinating time: 6–12 hours
Cooking time: 2 hours 30 minutes
Difficulty: ★

**Serves 4**

| | |
|---|---|
| 3½ lb/1.5 kg | shoulder of lamb |
| 8 strips/200 g | regular bacon |
| 5 | onions |
| 3 | carrots |
| 8 cloves | garlic |
| 2 | cloves |
| 2 | tomatoes |
| 2 | bay leaves |

| | |
|---|---|
| 2 | sprigs fresh rosemary |
| few sprigs | fresh thyme |
| ¼ bunch | fresh parsley |
| 10 | black peppercorns |
| 10 | white peppercorns |
| | zest of 1 orange |
| 1 pinch | grated nutmeg |
| 4 cups/1 l | dry white wine |
| 2 tbsp | sunflower oil |
| | salt |
| | pepper |

This is a classic recipe from Provence. Jean-Michel Minguella was given it by a chef friend. For the meat you should buy an especially nice shoulder of lamb. The more tightly it adheres to the bone, the more marked the flavor that it gives the stew.

*Daube*, Provençal lamb stew, was originally prepared with mutton, but over time it has been replaced by milder flavored lamb. Jean-Michel Minguella deviates from the usual preparation method, but brings new life to this famous casserole by using young, meadow-grazed lamb. He recommends lamb from the area around Sisteron.

If you can't find shoulder you could use neck of lamb instead. In any case the meat should be boned carefully. Keep the bones, because they add a lot of flavor to the dish. You can ask your butcher to chop the bones into small pieces.

To flavor the marinade, you can rely on the powerful flavor of thyme, by adding a few sprigs to the meat. Thyme is frequently used in lamb and mutton dishes. Apart from its antibacterial and aromatic properties, this herb is also part of a traditional bouquet garni. Strongly scented rosemary can become overpowering, so it's best to use just a small sprig.

To save time, Jean-Michel Minguella recommends that you prepare the marinade the day before you intend to cook the stew. The casserole takes a long time to cook anyway. He suggests sautéed potatoes as an accompaniment, but rice or pasta would also go well with this dish. It should be served piping hot.

*Remove as much fat as possible from the shoulder of lamb. Bone it, leaving a little meat on the bones. Retain the bones and cut the meat into 1½ oz/40 g chunks. Cut the bacon into pieces.*

*Peel the onions, carrots, and garlic. Spike one onion with 2 cloves. Finely dice the other onions, the carrots, and tomatoes.*

*Put the meat and bones in a large bowl with the diced carrots, onions and tomatoes, bay leaves, the whole onion spiked with cloves, 1 sprig rosemary, thyme, parsley, peppercorns, and orange zest. Season with salt and add grated nutmeg. Marinate in white wine for 6 hours.*

# Stew

Remove the orange zest from the marinade and reserve it. Remove the onion with the cloves. Fry the chopped bacon in 2 tbsp sunflower oil. Take the bacon out of the pan and reserve. Sauté the chopped onions and carrots from the marinade in the same pan and put aside.

Drain the meat and bones, reserving the strained marinade, and brown them in the pan.

Now put all the ingredients back into the pan, plus the orange zest. Pour the marinade over the meat and vegetables and simmer the casserole for around 2½ hours on low heat. Season to taste with salt and pepper, and serve piping hot with the accompaniment of your choice.

# Chicken Roulades

Preparation time:   1 hour
Cooking time:   1 hour 5 minutes
Difficulty:   ★★

**Serves 4**

| | |
|---|---|
| 1 | free-range chicken weighing 4 lb/1.7 kg |
| 4 | large shrimp |
| 4 | yellow onions |
| 1 tbsp | olive oil |
| | salt, pepper |

**For the shrimp sauce:**

| | |
|---|---|
| 4 | small shrimp |
| 1 | onion |
| 8 cloves | garlic |

| | |
|---|---|
| ⅓ cup + 1½ tbsp/ 100 ml | dark rum |
| ⅓ cup + 1½ tbsp/ 100 ml | vintage Banyuls |
| 6 tbsp | olive oil |
| | salt, pepper |

**For the chicken stock:**

| | |
|---|---|
| 1 | onion |
| 1 clove | garlic |
| 1 stick | celery |
| 1 | bay leaf |
| 1 sprig | thyme |
| 1 tbsp | olive oil |

**For the garnish:**

fresh chives (optional)

Catalans particularly love the combination of chicken and shellfish. Our recipe comes from Rosas, a little seaside resort close to the Spanish border, not far from Perpignan, and it is typical of the region, where the famous pink gambas are caught. Normally the shellfish are added directly to the chicken gravy, but our chef has changed the recipe by stuffing the chicken with the shrimp. He wanted to stress delicate flavors.

In France this dish is called *Dodine*. In the Middle Ages this term was used to describe a sauce based on chicken fat. Over the centuries the word developed, and is now pronounced more like the adjective *dodu*, meaning "plump." Nowadays a *dodine* is understood to be a small chicken roulade.

Depending on their diet, free-range chickens have delicate white or slightly yellowish flesh. Buy poultry with plump, firm flesh that is as lean as possible. Remember to remove the tendons at the bottom of the legs. Our chef advises cutting off the end of the roulade so that it can be stood upright on the plate. You could also prepare the dish with turkey breast.

Large shrimp have pride of place in this recipe from the coastal region. You can tell if they are fresh by how curved the shell is, whether the flesh is firm, and how easily they can be shelled. Remember to devein the shrimp. The chicken and shrimp should be tied together with kitchen thread so that they don't collapse during cooking. Do exactly the same if you use langoustines.

*Joint the chicken. Separate the thighs from the rump, removing the little back muscles. Cut along the breastbone to left and right, cutting off the breasts and wings. Cut off the tips of the wings. Bone the thighs completely. Reserve the bones and the chicken trimmings.*

*To make the chicken stock, brown the chicken trimmings and bones in olive oil. Add the diced onion and finely chopped garlic, chopped celery, bay leaf, and chopped thyme. Add enough water to cover the ingredients by about 2 in/5 cm and simmer for 30 minutes.*

*Shell the shrimp, leaving the heads on and season them. Wrap the pieces of chicken around the shrimp so that the shrimp's head is sticking out, then tie everything together tightly with kitchen string. Run a toothpick through the top of the shrimp's head and down through its body.*

# with Shrimp

Shrimp sauce: Sauté the small shrimp in 1 tbsp olive oil. Sweat the finely chopped onion with the shrimp, then add chopped garlic. Flambé the shrimp with rum and Banyuls, and simmer for 3 minutes. Add a generous ¾ cup/200 ml water. Season the sauce and simmer until reduced.

Strain the chicken stock. Poach the chicken and shrimp roulades in the stock at 340 °F/170 °C for 35 minutes. Remove the roulades and leave to cool. Save the stock. Sweat the 4 diced onions in olive oil for 25 minutes and put aside. Remove the string from the roulades.

Purée the shrimp sauce with a hand blender and pass it through a sieve. Add the reserved chicken stock, and beat in 5 tbsp olive oil. Arrange the roulades on a bed of caramelized onions, with the shrimp sauce. Garnish with chives.

# Stuffed Shoulder

| | |
|---|---|
| Preparation time: | *2 hours* |
| Cooking time: | *1 hour 10 minutes* |
| Difficulty: | ★★★ |

**Serves 4**

| | |
|---|---|
| 2 | rabbit torsos |
| 1 | onion |
| 2 cloves | garlic |
| 1 | carrot |
| 1 | bouquet garni (thyme, bay leaf, parsley) |
| generous ⅛ stick/ | |
| 20 g | butter |
| 1 cup/250 ml | dry white wine |
| 1 | pig's caul |
| ¼ stick/30 g | butter for frying |

**For the stuffing:**

| | |
|---|---|
| | rabbit liver and kidneys |
| 1 strip | back bacon |

| | |
|---|---|
| 2 oz/50 g | lean veal |
| 7 oz/200 g | button mushrooms |
| 1 | onion |
| 2 cloves | garlic |
| 1 bunch | fresh parsley |
| generous ⅛ stick/ | |
| 20 g | butter |
| | salt, pepper |

**For the apricot gypsy toast:**

| | |
|---|---|
| 2 tbsp | milk |
| 1 | egg |
| few sprigs | fresh rosemary |
| 1 | stale baguette |
| scant ⅛ stick/ | |
| 10 g | butter |
| 1 cup/200 g | dried apricots |

We have chef Alain Carro to thank for this recipe, which won a prize at the renowned Marseilles *Mangez du lapin* ("Eat Rabbit") competition in 1998. The unusual way in which the rabbit is filleted and the dual method of preparation – pan-fried and oven-roasted – will astound your friends.

Filleting the loin requires great care, and only in the case of superb quality rabbits are the bones sufficiently strong. Free-range rabbits, preferably from Angers, are best. It's even better if you buy only the front part of the rabbit. Our chef wraps the rabbit's shoulders in a pig's caul to keep them moist and help them retain their shape. If you can't obtain a pig's caul, you will need to hold the meat together with toothpicks.

The apricot gypsy toast adds a touch of acidity and a stylish, exotic, sweet-and-sour note. If you want to emphasize

this, our chef suggests you cook some orange zest with the gravy. These flavors are found throughout the Mediterranean region, especially in some Moroccan stews, known as *tajines*. Finally, rosemary grows throughout the Mediterranean region, wherever there is chalky soil and lots of sunshine. Where you find *garrigue*, the southern scrubland, rosemary will be there too.

If your guests particularly value attractive, colorful presentation, our chef suggests you garnish the plates with a sprig of cherry tomatoes. If they are briefly pan-fried, the skin swells upwards very elegantly.

*Separate the rabbit shoulders and bone out the shoulder blades. Carefully remove all the flesh from the bones, and spread it out for stuffing later. Reserve the head and bones.*

*Make an incision in the little loins and bone out the ends of the rib bones. Only cut through the first ribs again.*

*Sauté the rabbit bones and meat scraps, finely chopped onion, sliced garlic, chopped carrot, and bouquet garni in butter for 10 minutes. Add the white wine and let it evaporate. Add enough water to cover the meat and vegetables. Simmer for 15–20 minutes, then strain the gravy.*

# of Rabbit

To make the stuffing, dice the rabbit liver and kidneys, bacon, veal, and mushrooms. Peel and chop the onion and garlic, chop the parsley. Sauté them with the butter. Season with salt and pepper.

Stuff the rabbit shoulders and wrap them in the pig's caul. Sauté in an oven-proof skillet with a scant ⅛ stick/10 g butter for 5 minutes. Add the gravy, transfer to the oven, and roast the shoulders at 400° F/200 °C, basting regularly with the pan juices. Sauté the rabbit loins.

Beat together the milk, egg, and some chopped rosemary, and dip slices of bread in the egg mixture. Fry the egg-soaked bread in the butter. Top each slice of bread with sliced apricot and rosemary. Arrange the rabbit and toast on a plate. Pour gravy over the loins only.

# Perugine Sausages

Preparation time: 30 minutes
Cooking time: 35 minutes
Difficulty: ★★

**Serves 4**

| | |
|---|---|
| 2 | large onions |
| 2 tbsp | olive oil |
| 4 cloves | garlic |
| 8 | Perugine sausages |
| 4 | baby carrots |
| 1 bunch | scallions |

| | |
|---|---|
| 1 | shallot |
| scant ¾ stick/ 75 g | butter |
| 1¼ cups/250 g | Arborio rice |
| ⅓ cup/80 ml | white wine |
| 2 cups/500 ml | chicken stock |
| 10 oz/300 g | fresh peas |
| ¼ cup/50 g | grated parmesan |
| | salt |

Braised Perugine sausages are a specialty of Nice. In this recipe Daniel Ettlinger wanted to cross the Alpine border and therefore has chosen a typical Italian risotto as an accompaniment.

Perugine sausages are still made by hand. You don't need any additional pepper because of their spicy taste.

In the opinion of our chef, a risotto's success always depends on the quality of the rice and he therefore recommends the most suitable type, Italian Arborio. This high-quality rice has the advantage that the grains don't stick together during cooking. The risotto in our recipe is a gleaming, creamy white because of the butter and onions. As soon as the onions and rice turn translucent, add the white wine.

Watch the rice carefully during cooking. The chicken stock, which has to be added regularly, must be hot and added in the right quantities. Here's another useful tip from our chef: Rice should not be salted until three quarters of the way through the cooking time.

Risotto isn't risotto without parmesan. The king of Italian cheeses is a certified product from semi-skimmed cow's milk, which is heated into a malleable mass, pressed, and which develops a natural rind. It tastes slightly smoky (because of the lactic acid), fruity, salty, and sometimes rather piquant.

Peas are mainly cultivated in southwest France and are available from May. The pods should be a smooth, bright green. Peas are easy to shuck and need not be washed.

*Peel the onions and cut them into quarters. Sauté them in 1 tbsp olive oil, with the unpeeled garlic cloves, for 2–3 minutes.*

*Fry the Perugine sausages in the remaining olive oil for 5 minutes. Add the onions and garlic, and cook for 10 minutes. Add the carrots, cut into sticks, and sweat them with the sausages and onions for 10 minutes, then add the white of the scallions, reserving the green tops.*

*To make the risotto, sweat the finely chopped shallot in ½ stick/50 g butter for 5 minutes.*

# with Risotto

Add the rice and stir it until it is pearly and translucent. Deglaze the pan with the white wine. Add half the chicken stock.

Simmer the rice over low heat for 18 minutes, adding a ladleful of stock every few minutes. Shuck the peas and blanch them in boiling, salted water for around 6 minutes.

Fold the remaining butter and grated parmesan into the rice. Chop the scallion greens into rings, add to the risotto. Slice the sausages. Reheat the carrots and peas in the sausage fat. Arrange the risotto on a plate with the sausage slices, sautéed garlic, onions, carrots and peas.

# Haunch of Kid

Preparation time: 35 minutes
Time to
  freeze garlic: 10 minutes
Chichoumay
  cooking time: 30 minutes
Cooking time
  for meat: 60 minutes
Difficulty: ★

**Serves 4**

| | |
|---|---|
| 2 cloves | garlic |
| 3 lb/1.2 kg | haunch of kid/leg of lamb |
| 16 | juniper berries |
| 3 tbsp | olive oil |
| 1 | onion |
| 5 cloves | garlic |
| 2 sprigs | fresh thyme |
| | salt |
| | pepper |

**For the chichoumay:**

| | |
|---|---|
| 1 | eggplant |
| 1 | zucchini |
| 3 | tomatoes |
| 6 | scallions |
| 6 tbsp | regular olive oil |
| 2 cloves | garlic |
| 1 | bay leaf |
| 3 | basil leaves |
| 6 tbsp | highly aromatic olive oil |
| | salt, pepper |

Kid is very popular in the Languedoc region, especially meat from 7-week-old animals. The dish is dependent on the time of year and child's play to prepare; it's best between February and April.

Relatively firm, low-fat kid meat has a strong flavor. If you can't find kid, you could use leg of lamb instead. The juniper berries give the dish all the flavor of the *garrigue*, the perfumed scrubland of Languedoc. These aromatic berries, with their slightly resinous taste, grow on the thorny juniper bush. Juniper berries are a superb complement to game.

*Chichoumay* is ratatouille minus the bell peppers. The eggplant, which originated in India, had found a home in Provence as early as the 12th century. Choose fat, firm specimens. Because eggplant, like poisonous belladonna, is a member of the nightshade family, it was initially called *mala insana*, "unhealthy fruit." Nowadays eggplant is popular in combination with zucchini and tomatoes. If you can, buy tomatoes on the vine, available between June and October, as they have a better flavor.

The famous trio from southern French cuisine is completed by zucchini, which, like the marrow or cucumber, is a member of the pumpkin family. Baby zucchini are best; they should feel firm. The pumpkin is one of the oldest varieties of vegetable known. Once again it was the Italians who brought us this delicious vegetable. In the 18th century they hit on the idea of stewing unripe pumpkins ... and so the zucchini took its place in the kitchen.

Peel 2 cloves of garlic, cut them into slivers, and freeze them for 10 minutes in the deep freeze. Pierce the meat all over with a sharp knife, and insert the garlic slivers and juniper berries into the holes. Season the meat with salt and pepper.

Place the leg of lamb in a baking dish brushed with 2 tbsp olive oil. Preheat the oven to 350° F/180 °C. Add the finely chopped onion, whole unpeeled garlic cloves, and thyme to the meat, and roast it for 60 minutes. Turn the meat frequently and baste it with the pan juices.

Wash the eggplant and zucchini. Cut them into 1½ in/4 cm batons. Blanch each separately for 2–3 minutes and drain. Pour boiling water over the tomatoes, skin and deseed them, and dice the flesh. Wash the scallions and cut them into 1¼ in/4 cm pieces.

# on Chichoumay

Heat the regular olive oil in a pan. Fry the zucchini, eggplant, and scallions separately in the olive oil for 5 minutes each. Then put them all in the pan together.

Add 2 crushed cloves of garlic and the bay leaf to the vegetables and season. Sweat for 5 minutes (the vegetables should still be crisp). Toward the end of the cooking time add the diced tomato, finely chopped basil and aromatic olive oil. Sweat the vegetables for 5 minutes.

When the leg of lamb is done, take the baking dish out of the oven. Deglaze the dish with a little water. Just before serving, baste the meat again with the juices and a tablespoon of olive oil. Arrange the hot chichoumay around the lamb.

# Rabbit with

Preparation time: 1 hour 30 minutes
Cooking time: 1 hour
Difficulty: ★★

**Serves 4**

| | |
|---|---|
| 1 | rabbit weighing 3 lb/1.2 kg |
| 1 | red bell pepper |
| 1 | green bell pepper |
| generous ¾ cup/200 ml | olive oil |
| 1 can | peeled tomatoes |
| 2 sprigs | thyme |
| 5 | potatoes |

| | |
|---|---|
| 8 oz/250 g | green beans |
| ⅓ cup + 1½ tbsp/ 100 ml | milk |
| 2 cloves | garlic |
| 1 tbsp | chopped parsley |
| 8 oz/250 g | carrots |
| 1 | onion |
| 1 cup/250 ml | white wine |
| | salt |
| | pepper |

**For the garnish:**

| | |
|---|---|
| 4 sprigs | fresh thyme |
| 4 | vine tomatoes |

*Hachis parmentier* is a rustic French dish of chopped meat and potatoes. It takes its name from Antoine-Augustin Parmentier, a famous military doctor and agronomist. He made a significant contribution to the potato being recognized as a healthy, cheap, basic source of food. For a long time it was regarded as cattle fodder, or at best food for the poor. The olive oil gives the mashed potato flavor.

When you bone the rabbit, cut off all the fat. We recommend frying the liver and kidneys in advance, to obtain the juices. If you dust them with flour before frying them they will brown well, but they should stay nicely pink inside. Instead of rabbit you could use baby partridge for this recipe. To make it easier to prepare the meat, fry it first, then chop it. You should not use a food processor to do this, however, otherwise the meat will have an unpleasant consistency. Angel Yagues stresses that in this recipe it should be possible to identify the pieces of meat when mixed with the peppers.

Chop the bones to make the rabbit gravy. When you serve this dish, the gravy is poured over the variety meats.

Bell peppers are popular as a cooked vegetable and raw in salads. When you buy them make sure the skin is shiny. Thyme grows wild in the *garrigue*, the Languedoc scrubland. This tough, aromatic herb, with its little green-gray leaves, is picked in May and will keep for a whole year.

*Cut off the rabbit thighs using a meat cleaver. Bone the thighs carefully using a sharp knife. Reserve the rabbit's rump and all the bones for the gravy. Refrigerate the thigh meat, liver, and kidneys.*

*Wash, core, and very finely dice the bell peppers. Sweat them in a little olive oil. Drain the can of peeled tomatoes and reserve the juice. Add the tomatoes with a sprig of thyme, and simmer for approximately 10 minutes. Crush the mixture with a spatula.*

*Wash and peel the potatoes. Place them in cold, salted water, bring them to the boil, and simmer for about 20 minutes. Boil the green beans in salted water for 8 minutes. Drain the potatoes and mash them with the milk. Beat in 5 tbsp olive oil and season with salt and pepper.*

# Thyme

Chop the rabbit meat. Cut the kidneys in half lengthwise and fry them, with the liver, in 1 tbsp olive oil for 5 minutes. Fry the meat in the same pan for 5 minutes. Season with salt and pepper. Add the chopped garlic, chopped parsley, and a sprig of thyme.

To make the gravy, brown the rabbit bones and rump in 1 tbsp olive oil. Add the diced carrots, finely chopped onion, and other sprig of thyme. Deglaze the pan with the white wine. Add the tomato juice. Simmer the gravy for 20 minutes, strain it, and season with salt and pepper.

Using a ring mold, layer the chopped meat, tomato and bell pepper mix, and mashed potato. Arrange the sliced kidneys and liver, green beans, and cooked vine tomatoes on the plate. Pour the gravy over the variety meats, and garnish with a sprig of thyme.

| | |
|---|---|
| *Preparation time:* | *1 hour* |
| *Cooking time:* | *25 minutes* |
| *Difficulty:* | ★★ |

**Serves 4**

| | |
|---|---|
| 2 | pigeons, each 1 lb/500 g |
| 3 tbsp | olive oil |
| 1 | medium onion, peeled, (keep skin) |
| 2 sprigs | fresh thyme |
| ⅔ cup/150 ml | chicken stock |
| 4 | medium new potatoes |
| 4 | baby carrots |

| | |
|---|---|
| 5 oz/150 g | peas, shucked |
| 5 oz/150 g | fava beans, shucked |
| | rock salt |
| | salt, pepper |

**For the stuffing:**

| | |
|---|---|
| 2 slices | baguette, cubed |
| ⅓ cup + 1½ tbsp/ 100 ml | milk |
| 1 | small onion |
| 1 tbsp | olive oil |
| 4 cloves | garlic |
| 2 | Perugine sausages |
| 1 bunch | fresh flat-leaf parsley |
| 1 sprig | fresh thyme |
| | salt |

Stuffed pigeon on a bed of seasonal vegetables is a rustic dish from the area around Nice. Originally it was cooked simply, braised over low heat. In our chef's recipe it gets a spicy filling.

Tender, tasty pigeon makes a delicious meal of this poultry dish. Wild pigeon is available from spring to the end of summer; the rest of the year farmed pigeon is on the market. If you have difficulty jointing the pigeon, ask your butcher to remove the wings from the body. You need the tips of the wings and the rump, though, for the gravy. Daniel Ettlinger advises leaving the pigeon to rest for a few minutes before removing the fillets. Put the stuffed pigeon carefully in the pan so the skin doesn't tear.

The stuffing must cool a little before inserting it under the pigeon skin. The stuffing gets its characteristic taste from the slightly spicy Perugine sausages, so you don't need any additional pepper. Before making the stuffing, you should remove the skin from the sausage. Then, when you sauté it, it will marry with the other stuffing ingredients and be cooked at the same time as the pigeon. The cubed bread must be softened thoroughly in the milk so that it is easy to incorporate into the stuffing. Keep the onion skin for the gravy.

The accompanying vegetables are dependent upon the time of year. In spring you could use tender fava beans in the pod, you could also use sugar snap peas, or green beans. Salt the vegetables at the start of cooking, so they retain their color. In winter you could serve turnip or chicory if available.

*Soak the cubed bread in the milk. Peel and dice the small onion and sweat it in 1 tbsp olive oil. Stir in the finely chopped garlic, Perugine sausages, softened, drained bread, chopped parsley, and thyme. Season the mixture with salt.*

*Take the wings off the pigeon without damaging the skin on the breast. Cut off the wing tips and fillet the breast. To do this, cut along each side of the breastbone.*

*With your finger, gently ease the skin away from the meat and insert the stuffing. Reshape the pigeon breast.*

# Seasonal Vegetables

Sauté the bones and wings in 1 tbsp olive oil, and season them with salt. Add the onion skin with 1 sprig thyme, and sweat them for 10 minutes. Deglaze the pan with the chicken stock. After 10 minutes, remove the wings and simmer for another 15 minutes. Strain the gravy.

Sauté the peeled and quartered potatoes and sliced onion in 1 tbsp olive oil for 5 minutes. Season with salt and pepper. Add the remaining sprig of thyme, as well as the carrot sticks, and sweat them for 10 minutes.

Blanch the peas in boiling water, salted with rock salt, for 6 minutes. Add the peas and the beans to the other vegetables. Roast the pigeon in the remaining olive oil at 465 °F/250 °C. Let the pigeon rest for 3 minutes. Arrange the pigeon on a plate with the vegetables and gravy.

# Guinea Fowl

Preparation time:    15 minutes
Cooking time:    1 hour
Difficulty:    ★★

**Serves 4**

| | |
|---|---|
| 1 | free-range guinea fowl |
| 4 strips | back bacon |
| 1 tbsp | olive oil |
| 3 | unwaxed lemons |
| 3½ tbsp/50 ml | Banyuls (or other fortified wine) |
| ¾ cup/200 ml | veal stock |

| | |
|---|---|
| | zest of 1 Seville orange |
| 30 cloves | garlic |
| | salt |
| | pepper |

**For the bouquet garni:**
    fresh thyme
    bay leaf
    fresh parsley

**For the garnish:**
    fresh chives

If you open any Catalan cookery book, you're sure to find this recipe, which was originally prepared with partridge. Our chef recommends that you buy a free-range guinea fowl, then you can be sure that this classic bird will have firm, tasty flesh.

The meat of these birds is most delicious when they are very young, and guinea fowl are available all year round. In Europe, most of them come from France or Italy. The guinea fowl reached France from Rome, and from there spread all over Europe to wherever there is a temperate climate. Jean Plouzennec wraps strips of bacon around the guinea fowl to prevent the meat from drying out. This is made from belly pork that is soaked in brine for around ten days, then rubbed with pepper, and hung up to dry.

Banyuls is a sweet dessert wine (*vin doux naturel*) whose fermentation is stopped by adding alcohol, so that the

grapey flavor and sweetness are maintained. Together with the acidic orange zest, it gives the sweet-and-sour taste common to many Catalan gravies.

The main areas of lemon cultivation in Europe are found in Italy and on the Iberian peninsula, but they are also cultivated in the south of France, mainly in Menton. Buy relatively large fruit with a deep yellow color.

Sticking with tradition, you could prepare this dish with the best young partridge joints, which are more tender than older birds. Allow one baby partridge per person. The meat is a slightly grayish color. New potatoes and, depending on the season, boletus (porcini) or chanterelle mushrooms are a suitable accompaniment.

*Preheat the oven to 400 °F/200 °C. Season the guinea fowl inside, and out. Wrap bacon around both thighs. Lay the remaining strips of bacon on the breast, and tie the legs together with kitchen thread. Drizzle olive oil over the guinea fowl and roast for 35–40 minutes.*

*Baste the guinea fowl with the juices throughout cooking. Remove the peel from the lemons in one piece and remove the pith. Fillet two lemons into segments, and slice the third.*

*Remove the bacon from the guinea fowl and put aside. Joint the guinea fowl in the classic manner, separating the thighs, breasts, and wings (cut through the latter). For the gravy, put the carcass back into the roasting pan. Deglaze the pan with the Banyuls and the veal stock.*

# with Garlic

Add the bouquet garni and the orange zest, season with salt and pepper, and simmer for about 10 minutes. Strain the gravy through a sieve, making sure you squeeze out all the goodness.

Blanch the whole cloves of garlic twice in boiling water. Add them to the gravy with the lemon segments. Bring to the boil, cover, and simmer for 10 minutes. Add the sliced lemon and season to taste with salt and pepper.

Add the guinea fowl joints to the gravy and heat them through. Arrange the guinea fowl joints on a plate with the lemon slices, bacon strips, and garlic cloves. Garnish with a couple of blades of chives.

# Fillet of Beef with

Preparation time:    1 hour
Time for soaking
     the bones:    24 hours
Time for resting
     the batter:    1 hour
Cooking time:    1 hour
Difficulty:    ★★

**Serves 4**

| | |
|---|---|
| 20 | fresh anchovies |
| | oil for frying |
| 12 pieces | bone marrow |
| 2 cloves | garlic |
| 1 sprig | fresh thyme |
| 1 | bay leaf |
| 4 slices | fillet of beef |
| | weighing 6 oz/180 g |
| 2 tbsp | olive oil |
| ¾ cup/200 ml | red wine |
| ¾ cup/200 ml | port |

| | |
|---|---|
| 1⅔ cups/400 ml | beef stock |
| | salt, pepper |

**For the tempura batter:**

| | |
|---|---|
| ¼ cup/30 g | all-purpose flour |
| 10 | ice cubes |
| | salt |
| | pepper |

**For the pissaladière dough:**

| | |
|---|---|
| 1 tsp/5 g | salt |
| 1 envelope/5 g | active dry yeast |
| 2⅛ cups/250 g | all-purpose flour |
| 1 | small egg |

**For the topping:**

| | |
|---|---|
| 2¼ lb/1 kg | onions |
| ⅓ cup + 1½ tbsp/ | |
| 100 ml | olive oil |
| | fresh thyme |
| | bay leaf |
| | fresh parsley |
| 4 | anchovies in oil |
| 1 | tomato |
| 8 | black olives |
| | salt, pepper |

**For the garnish:**

| | |
|---|---|
| | fresh parsley |
| | rock salt |

Nice and its *pissaladière*! This flatbread, lavishly topped with anchovy fillets and black olives, whose name dates back to the 14th century, is equally tasty hot or cold. Originally, before it was baked in the oven, it was spread with *pissalat*, a Provençal seasoning paste that is made with puréed anchovies, thyme, star anise, bay leaves, pepper, and olive oil.

The first main ingredient in Laurent Broussier's original recipe is the anchovies. These saltwater fish, a maximum of 8 inches/20 centimeters long, have yellowish-green backs and silvery bellies. If you use fresh fish that take a little longer to cook, buy ready-filleted fish. Preserved sardines are already salted, so remember this when seasoning your dish.

To make the *pissaladière* dough you will need around ⅔ cup/150 milliliters of water. Put half into one container with the salt, and the other half into another with the yeast. Make a circle of flour on the work surface. Put the egg in the middle, with the salt water, and yeast water. Knead the dough by hand until it no longer sticks to your fingers. Then leave it to rest for an hour. If you don't want to go to the trouble of making the dough, bought bread rolls are an alternative.

Soak the bone marrow well so that any blood and toxins are eliminated. The marrow is heated through again briefly just before serving. The marrow is served sprinkled with rock salt and chopped parsley.

*To make the tempura batter, put the flour and ice cubes in a bowl. Beat with a whisk until the ice cubes have melted and a fluid batter has formed. Season the batter with salt and pepper.*

*If making the pissaladière dough, see above. Shape it into rolls. Bake for 20 minutes at 425 °F/220°C. To make the topping, peel the onions and slice them into rings. Sweat them gently in some olive oil. Add the chopped thyme and season sparingly.*

*Add the bay leaf, roughly chopped parsley and anchovy fillets. Sweat over low heat for 30 minutes until the anchovy fillets have melted. Add the diced tomato and season with salt and pepper.*

# Tempura Anchovies

Immerse the fresh anchovies in the tempura batter and fry them for 1 minute in very hot fat. Drain them on kitchen paper.

Slice the bread rolls in half and toast them. Layer the onion mixture, olives, and fried anchovies on the bottom half of the roll, and top with the other half.

Poach the bone marrow in salted water with pepper, garlic, thyme, and bay leaf for 3–4 minutes. Fry the fillets of beef in olive oil. Take the fillets out of the pan and deglaze it with the red wine and port. Add the beef stock, stirring all the time, and boil until reduced by one third.

# Pigeon and

Preparation time: 55 minutes
Cooking time: 1 hour 5 minutes
Difficulty: ★★

**Serves 4**

| | |
|---|---|
| 2 | pigeons, each 1 lb/500 g |
| 1 stick/100 g | butter |
| 2 | shallots |
| ⅔ cup/150 ml | port |
| 4 | carrots |
| | rock salt |
| 2 | shallots |
| 1 clove | garlic |
| 1½ cups/300 g | Arborio rice |

generous ¾ cup/
200 ml
scant ½ cup/100 g

chicken stock
parmesan

| | |
|---|---|
| 1 sprig | flat-leaf parsley |
| 6 oz/160 g | chanterelles |
| 3 tbsp | olive oil |
| | salt, pepper |

**For the pigeon gravy:**

| | |
|---|---|
| 1 | carrot |
| 1 stick | celery |
| 1 | onion |
| generous ⅛ stick/ | |
| 20 g | butter |
| ⅓ cup + 1½ tbsp/ | |
| 100 ml | red wine |
| ⅓ cup + 1½ tbsp/ | |
| 100 ml | chicken stock |
| 1 | bay leaf |
| 1 sprig | fresh thyme |

Joël Garault works in Monte Carlo. His recipe is a homage to the *Gallia Transalpina* of antiquity. The risotto is directly connected with Italy and the other ingredients come from the department of Alpes-de-Haute-Provence.

Wild pigeons are available from spring to the end of summer, the rest of the year you can buy farmed pigeons. When jointing the pigeon, remember to reserve the wing tips and rump, as you need them to make the gravy. You could also use quail or baby guinea fowl in this recipe.

The yellow chanterelle mushrooms give this dish a special Provençal flavor. These mushrooms are available from June until the fall. In damp weather they flourish in the Provençal countryside and their delicious scent is reminiscent of apricots. Garnish the chanterelle mushrooms with a little chopped parsley.

Joël Garault values Italian cuisine. He uses Arborio rice for his risotto. This high-quality rice has the advantage that the grains don't stick together when cooked. If you want to make this dish a little richer, add puréed garlic braised in olive oil to the risotto, but still add the butter and the parmesan cheese.

In our recipe, the parmesan is in the form of chips baked on a non-stick baking sheet. The king of Italian cheeses is a certified product from semi-skimmed cow's milk, which is heated into a malleable mass, pressed, and which develops a natural rind. It tastes slightly smoky (because of the lactic acid), fruity, salty, and sometimes piquant.

*Separate the pigeon thighs with a knife by cutting through the joint. Take off the legs and wings. Take out the spine and breastbone, and keep all the trimmings and bones for the gravy.*

*To make the gravy, finely dice the carrot, celery and onion. Fry the pigeon rump and scraps in butter. Add the vegetables and sauté them with the pigeon. Add the red wine and leave it to evaporate completely. Add the chicken stock, bay leaf, and thyme, and simmer for 25 minutes.*

*Sauté the pigeon thighs in a generous ⅛ stick/20 g butter. When they are golden brown, add 2 sliced shallots. Deglaze the pan with the port and reduce the liquid. Strain the gravy and add it to the pan. Simmer for 25 minutes. Take the thighs out of the pan and strain the sauce.*

# Chanterelle Risotto

Peel the carrots and boil them for 1 minute in water salted with rock salt. Drain the carrots, and slice them so they form a fan shape. Peel and finely chop 2 shallots and the garlic. Sweat them in a pan with ½ stick/50 g butter. Stir in the rice.

To make the risotto, add the chicken stock and simmer for 15 minutes. Fold in ¼ stick/30 g butter and 4 tsp parmesan. Season and add the chopped parsley, reserving a little for the garnish. Spoon the remaining parmesan on a baking sheet. Broil so that it melts to form chips.

Sauté the chanterelles for a few minutes. Season the pigeon, fry it for 3 minutes on each side, then bake it for 3 minutes at 350 °F/180 °C. Remove the fillets, slice them diagonally. Arrange the fillets with the thighs, chanterelles, and parmesan chips. Pour the sauce over the top.

# Desserts & Pastries

# Crème Brûlée

| | |
|---|---|
| Preparation time: | 40 minutes |
| Time for custard to cool: | 3 hours |
| Cooking time: | 2 hours 20 minutes |
| Difficulty: | ★ |

**Serves 4**

| | |
|---|---|
| ¾ cup/200 ml | Muscatel wine |
| 8 oz/250 g | white Muscatel grapes |

**For the crème brûlée:**

| | |
|---|---|
| 2 cups/500 ml | milk |
| 1 | vanilla bean |
| 1 tsp | vanilla extract |

| | |
|---|---|
| 6 | egg yolks |
| ⅔ cup/150 g | superfine sugar |
| | confectioner's sugar |

**For the vanilla ice cream:**

| | |
|---|---|
| 1 cup/250 ml | milk |
| 4 | egg yolks |
| scant ½ cup/ 100 g | superfine sugar |
| 1 tbsp | vanilla extract |

**For the garnish:**

| | |
|---|---|
| 1 punnet | raspberries |
| | redcurrants |
| | fresh mint |

Crème brûlée with Muscatel wine is a typical dessert from the Languedoc region, where the grapes for this sweet white wine ripen in vineyards on slopes below the Mediterranean scrub. It is drunk as an aperitif and is also popular for use in cooking. The grapes grow in small bunches with pale, perfumed, firm berries. When preparing this dish, the grapes are skinned and deseeded before being heated briefly in the wine. You could use a dessert wine such as Beaumes de Venise, or a liqueur such as Grand Marnier or Cointreau, in this easy-to-prepare dessert instead.

During cooking, the aluminum foil prevents the water from boiling. To save time, our chef recommends that you prepare the custard a day in advance.

Vanilla is the dominant flavor in this recipe. The vanilla bean, whose essence is used, is a climbing plant from the orchid family. It was originally cultivated in Mexico, but now grows in the Antilles, in Madagascar, and on the Comoro Islands. The ripe vanilla beans are harvested, boiled in water, and then dried in the sun. In the process they turn dark brown and are covered in a layer of crystals that look like frost, which is what gives vanilla its characteristic perfume and flavor.

The Muscatel wine sauce is made using melted vanilla ice cream, but really it's a crème anglaise, or custard. To make it, bring the milk to the boil. Beat together the egg yolks and sugar until frothy, then fold in the vanilla extract. Pour on the hot milk and mix well. Return the mixture to the pan and simmer for two minutes, then pour it into a container and put it in the freezer. If you're short of time you could melt ready-made vanilla ice cream to make the sauce.

*To make the crème brûlée, put the vanilla bean and the extract in the hot milk, and leave to infuse for 15 minutes. Strain the milk.*

*Beat together the egg yolks and sugar until very frothy. Pour on the flavored hot milk and mix well. Strain through a sieve.*

*Pour the mixture into ramekins. Line a deep baking sheet with aluminum foil, pour a little water into the base of the sheet, and place the ramekins on the baking sheet. Bake the custards for 2 hours at 250 °F/120 °C until set.*

# with Muscatel Wine

Pour the wine into a saucepan and add the skinned and deseeded grapes. Heat gently for 2 minutes, so that the grapes are infused with the flavor of the wine. Then remove the grapes and reserve for the garnish.

Run the tip of a knife carefully around the rim of the ramekins and turn out the custards onto a plate. Sprinkle confectioner's sugar over the top of the custards and cook under the broiler at 465 °F/250 °C.

Let the wine cool a little, then add the vanilla ice cream (see above for method). When the ice cream has melted completely, spoon a pool of sauce around the custards. Garnish with the Muscatel grapes, raspberries, redcurrants, and mint leaves.

# Catalan Custard

| | | | | |
|---|---|---|---|---|
| Preparation time: | 30 minutes | | | |
| Resting time: | 5–6 hours | | | |
| Time to cook | | | | |
| custard: | 20 minutes | | | |
| Time to cook | | | | |
| the panallets: | 1 hour 10 minutes | | | |
| Time to cook | | | | |
| the bunyètes: | 5 minutes | | | |
| Difficulty: | ★ | | | |

**Serves 4**

**For the Catalan custard:**

| | |
|---|---|
| 2 cups/500 ml | milk |
| generous ¾ cup/ | |
| 180 g | superfine sugar |
| 1¼ cups/150 g | ground almonds |
| 2 cups/500 ml | heavy cream |
| | zest of 1 orange |
| | zest of 1 lemon |
| 1 | cinnamon stick |
| 14 | egg yolks |
| 8 tbsp | raw cane sugar |

**For the bunyètes:**

| | |
|---|---|
| 2 | lemons |
| 10 cups/1 kg | flour |
| 2¼ sticks/250 g | butter, softened |
| 8 | eggs |
| 3 tbsp | orange flower water |
| 1 tbsp | sugar |
| 1 tbsp | oil + oil for frying |

**For the panallets:**

| | |
|---|---|
| 1 | sweet potato weighing 10 oz/300 g |
| 2 generous cups/ 250 g | ground almonds |
| 2¼ cups/250 g | confectioner's sugar |
| 1 cup/100 g | potato starch |
| 1 | egg, separated |
| ½ cup/100 g | pine nuts |

Here is the recipe for Catalan cuisine's global ambassador, an internationally renowned dessert. Of course you will also find it on the dessert menu of Jean Plouzennec's "Restaurant du Casino" in Amélie-les-Bains.

The recipe that we present here is accompanied by two classic recipes for cookies that every Catalan mother passes on to her children. Jean Plouzennec was bequeathed these famous recipes by his grandparents. Just before serving, the delicious Catalan custard is sprinkled with light brown sugar and broiled or brûléed with a cook's blow torch.

Cream is also part of this southern French recipe, which is explained by the fact that dairy farming has always been important in the Pyrenees. Cream and butter have been reserved predominantly for cakes and pastries in Catalan cuisine. Olive oil is almost always used for cooking.

The orange and lemon zests play an important role in this recipe, so make sure that you buy organic, unwaxed fruit. Chemical residues may remain even after the skin has been washed.

The *bunyètes*, crisp, sweet pancakes from the eastern Pyrenees get their wonderful flavor from the orange flower water. The best *bunyètes* have lots of air bubbles. The *panallets*, little pine nut-coated cookies, are eaten on All Saints' Day. The mashed sweet potato must have dried out thoroughly before it is folded into the almonds and sugar, and the mixture is shaped into balls.

*Bring the milk to the boil with 6 tbsp/90 g sugar. Add the ground almonds and take the pan off the heat. Leave the milk to infuse for a few minutes. Then add the cream and bring to the boil again.*

*Add the orange and lemon zests, as well as the cinnamon stick, broken into small pieces. Take the pan off the heat again and leave everything to infuse for around 5 minutes.*

*Put 14 egg yolks into a large bowl with the remaining sugar and beat well until foaming.*

# with Cookies

Add 2 large tbsp strained hot almond milk to the egg mixture, mixing well. Transfer to a saucepan, and cook gently on a low heat until a custard forms. Pour the custard into ramekins and refrigerate. Before serving, sprinkle over raw cane sugar and caramelize under a hot broiler.

To make the bunyètes, grate the zest of one lemon. Make a well in the flour, add the softened butter, eggs, grated lemon zest, orange flower water, sugar, and oil. Knead to form dough. Let the dough rest for 5–6 hours. Roll pieces of dough into thin circles and fry them in oil.

Panallets: Bake the sweet potato in foil for 1 hour at 350 °F/180 °C. Mix the mashed flesh with the almonds and sugar. Shape into balls, sprinkle with potato starch, dip in egg white, and coat in pine nuts. Brush with beaten egg yolk and bake for 10 minutes at 400 °F/200 °C.

# Figs in Red Wine

Preparation time:    30 minutes
Cooking time:        30 minutes
Difficulty:          ★

**Serves 4**

| | |
|---|---|
| 8 | figs |
| ⅔ cup/150 ml | red wine |
| ⅔ cup/150 ml | port |
| 5 generous tbsp/70 g | superfine sugar |
| 1 pinch | cinnamon |
| 1 | lemon |

| | |
|---|---|
| 1 | orange |
| ½ | vanilla bean |
| ½ lb/250 g | mascarpone |
| 2 | meringues |

This is a very simple recipe from the Nice area. The only thing about it that is difficult is choosing the figs which, as our chef stresses, do not keep well. They can only be stored for a day in the refrigerator. When they are ripe, small cracks appear in the surface and when you squeeze them gently with your fingers they give a little. They should definitely not be overripe though. A fresh stalk is an indication of fresh fruit. Daniel Ettlinger recommends the Belonne variety, which is especially sweet. When the figs are cooked in port the flavors soften a little. This fortified wine, whose fermentation is stopped by the additional of alcohol, is a popular aperitif. A sweet dessert wine (Banyuls or Beaumes de Venise) can also be used.

Cinnamon is also important in this recipe. This spice is obtained from the bark of an exotic shrub and in this case is used when poaching the fruit. Cinnamon is recognizable by its sweetish, pervasive aroma and piquant flavor.

On the Côte d'Azur, which is imbued with Italian culture, mascarpone is a popular ingredient. Lovers of tiramisu are likely to be familiar with this rich cheese. You could use heavy cream instead.

The figs poached in red wine with mascarpone cream are sprinkled with crushed meringue. To make meringues, egg whites are beaten together with lots of sugar until very stiff, and dried in the oven. Depending on how long they are baked, the meringues can be squishy, soft, or crisp. If you buy meringues, choose the crisp type.

This dessert takes little time to prepare, but our chef stresses that it should then be served immediately for perfect results.

*Wash the figs and carefully make a cross-shaped incision in the top with a small sharp knife.*

*Place the figs in a shallow baking dish and add the red wine and port.*

*Sprinkle over 3 heaped tbsp/50 g superfine sugar and a pinch of cinnamon.*

# with Mascarpone

Cut the lemon and orange into quarters, slit open the vanilla bean, and scrape out the seeds. Add one orange and one lemon quarter, and the vanilla seeds, to the figs. Bake the figs in the oven for 30 minutes at 400 °F/200 °C.

Beat together the mascarpone and remaining sugar.

Pour the wine from the baked figs into a deep plate. Arrange scoops of mascarpone in the sauce. Slice the figs in half and arrange 4 fig halves on each plate. Sprinkle crushed meringues over the top and garnish with the remaining orange and lemon quarters.

# Goat Milk Cheese

Preparation time:    15 minutes
Cooking time:        40 minutes
Difficulty:          ★

**Serves 4**

| | |
|---|---|
| 1 | eggplant |
| ⅝ cup/140 g | sugar |
| 7 oz/200 g | carrots |
| ⅓ cup + 1½ tbsp/100 ml | milk |
| 1 | vanilla bean |
| 2 tbsp/70 g | rosemary honey |

| | |
|---|---|
| 4 | young soft goat milk cheeses, each 5 oz/120 g |

**For the garnish:**
few sprigs   flowering rosemary

*Mel y mato* is Catalan for "honey and soft cheese." Jean-Claude Vila has taken his inspiration from this traditional recipe and changed it a little. "I have discovered that some vegetables taste wonderful with sugar, which is why I use eggplant and carrot in my recipe."

The goat milk cheese should be at least 45 percent fat. Its very bland taste is similar to that of soft cheese made from cow's milk. For this recipe buy four individual cheeses, each weighing around 5 ounces/120 grams.

This dessert is sweetened by honey, described in ancient times as the food of the gods. Honey, made by bees from the nectar in flowers, is stored in the honeycomb cells. Honey provides much more energy than sugar. The bees produce rosemary honey from the flowers of this Mediterranean herb that flourishes in the Catalan region. In addition, our chef uses rosemary as a garnish.

Preparing carrots with sugar is a sure-fire way to bring many a child round to liking this vegetable, which contains a lot of vitamin A. Buy fresh baby carrots if you are able, and adjust the cooking time according to the size and the quality.

Don't forget to keep the vanilla bean. After using it in this recipe, slit it open lengthwise, scrape out the seeds, and add them to the carrot and honey mixture.

The eggplant slices also make this recipe one of our chef's signature dishes. Beautifully crisp, as they are in this recipe, they make an ideal accompaniment and garnish on the plate.

*Wash the eggplant and carefully slice it thinly lengthwise.*

*To make the syrup, bring 1 cup/250 ml water to the boil with the sugar. Soak the eggplant slices in the hot syrup for about 3 minutes.*

*Drain the eggplant slices a little and spread them on a baking sheet lined with baking parchment. Bake them in the oven for around 8 minutes, at 340 °/170 °C, until browned.*

# with Honey

Put the peeled and sliced carrots into a saucepan with the milk, 1 cup + 1½ tbsp/100 ml water, and the vanilla bean. Boil, cover, and simmer for 15 minutes. Then take off the lid and continue cooking until the liquid has evaporated. Purée the carrots, then add the vanilla seeds.

Stir 1 level tbsp/30 g rosemary honey into the puréed carrot and cook on low heat for about 10 minutes.

Arrange the drained goat milk cheeses on a plate. Garnish with sprigs of flowering rosemary. Warm the remaining rosemary honey and drizzle it over the cheeses. Arrange a spoonful of puréed carrot and caramelized eggplant slices next to the cheese.

# Canebière

Preparation time:    1 hour
Cooling time:    1 hour 30 minutes
Cooking time:    15 minutes
Difficulty:    ★★

**Serves 4**

| 4 | physalis |
|---|---|

**For the caramel base:**

| ⅓ oz/10 g | semisweet chocolate |
|---|---|
| 1 tsp/5 g | cocoa butter |
| 3 oz/80 g | nougat |
| 3½ oz/100 g | wafers |

**For the liquorice mousse:**

| 2 | egg yolks |
|---|---|
| 3 tbsp/50 g | superfine sugar |

| 1 dash | liquorice extract |
|---|---|
| 2 envelopes | gelatin |
| ¾ cup/200 ml | heavy cream |

**For the Italian meringue:**

| 2 | egg whites |
|---|---|
| 3 scant tbsp/40 g | superfine sugar |

**For the chocolate mousse:**

| ¾ cup/200 ml | heavy cream |
|---|---|
| 3 tbsp/50 g | superfine sugar |
| 1 | egg yolk |
| 3½ oz/90 g | milk chocolate |
| 1½ oz/40 g | semisweet chocolate |

**For the custard with liquorice:**

| 2 | egg yolks |
|---|---|
| 3 tbsp/50 g | superfine sugar |
| 2 cups/500 ml | milk |
| 1 drop | liquorice extract |

This dessert is a specialty of the "Miramar," Jean-Michel Minguella's restaurant. His pastry chef, Fabrice Vaquer, created this delicious dessert and named it in honor of a famous avenue, the Canebière, which runs through Marseilles and terminates at the Old Harbor. Our dessert's name is a reminder that it was once a cobbled road.

This delicious liquorice-flavored dessert incorporates part of the city's history. In the past there was a liquorice factory not far from Avenue Canebière. Did you know that liquorice is obtained from a bush? The roots are called liquorice and are also available as sticks that can be chewed. The extract obtained from the bush is used to flavor alcohol and beer, and for liquorice candy. Because the flavor is very strong, you should use it extremely sparingly and ensure that it doesn't slip from your hands when you are adding it to a dish.

All the flavors that one might encounter when dining at the "Miramar" are connected with the port city. Every element in this dessert recreates the ancient city, and the chocolate adds an exotic, cosmopolitan note.

Physalis, the fruit that crowns this dessert, originates from Peru and is sometimes also known as Cape gooseberry. Depending on the time of year, you could use other acidic fruit such as star fruit, kiwi fruit, or pineapple. Jean-Michel Minguella has chosen physalis not just for the beauty of the orange berries, but also because of the delicate acidity which revives the taste buds after the sweetness of the sugar. The acidity balances the chocolate and the sweetness of the dessert.

*Melt the chocolate, cocoa butter, and nougat. Custard: Beat together the egg yolks and sugar until foamy. Heat the milk and add half of it to the egg mixture. Heat the other half on low heat, stirring all the time, until it boils. Then add the liquorice extract.*

*Pour the custard through a sieve and refrigerate it. Crumble the wafers and add them to the chocolate and nougat mixture. Spread this mixture over baking parchment until it is about ¼ in/½ mm thick. Put it in the freezer for 10 minutes to set.*

*Liquorice mousse: Beat the egg yolks and sugar until foamy. Add the liquorice extract and the gelatin dissolved in 2 tbsp hot water. Meringues: Beat the whites until very stiff. Heat ⅓ cup + 1½ tbsp/100 ml water and the sugar to 250 °F/120 °C. Slowly beat the syrup into the egg whites.*

# "Cobblestones"

Fold the meringue mixture into the liquorice mousse. Add the stiffly beaten cream and spread the mixture over the chocolate nougat mixture. Freeze for about 20 minutes.

Chocolate mousse: Beat the cream until stiff and put aside. Melt the sugar (230 °F/110 °C) and beat into the beaten egg yolk, using a hand mixer, then let it cool. Melt the milk and semisweet chocolate separately in double boilers or bowls over a saucepan of simmering water.

Mix the chocolate into the egg and sugar mixture, then carefully fold in the beaten cream. Spread this over the set liquorice mousse. Refrigerate for 1 hour. Pour some of the custard into a deep plate. Cut out four "cobblestones," from the set dessert and garnish each with a physalis.

# Nougat Mazarin

Preparation time: 1 hour
Cooling time: at least 5 hours
Cooking time: 15 minutes
Difficulty: ★

**Serves 4**

**For the nougat mazarin:**
| | |
|---|---|
| 4 | egg yolks |
| 3 tbsp/45 g | superfine sugar |
| 2 cups/500 ml | heavy cream |
| 5 oz/150 g | nougat |
| 2 oz/50 g | wafers |

**For the chopped nut topping:**
| | |
|---|---|
| ⅔ cup/150 g | superfine sugar |
| | juice of 1 lemon |
| scant ¾ cup/ 100 g | chopped almonds |

**For the chocolate frosting:**
| | |
|---|---|
| 3 ½ oz/100 g | semisweet chocolate (70% cocoa solids) |

**For the mango coulis:**
| | |
|---|---|
| 1 | ripe mango |
| 1 ¼ cups/300 ml | Grand Marnier |

**For the garnish:**
| | |
|---|---|
| 2 | kiwi fruit |

This sweet, melting dessert has nothing in common with the tough Cardinal Mazarin, one of the most important men at the time of Louis XIV. When pastry chefs refer to a *mazarin*, they mean a cake with two bases, with a *dacquoise* – a layer of egg white, almonds, and sugar – between the meringue and the sponge, and with a layer of nougat cream. Previously, Genoese sponge filled with fruit preserved in syrup was also called a *mazarin*.

Alain Carro's dessert must rest overnight in the freezer, or for a minimum of five hours, before serving. In 1997 our chef won the *Académie des glaces* competition in Paris with this recipe. It's so easy to make, a child could do it, but you should supervise making the caramel, and not leave it to a junior pastry chef.

Not only is this a delicious dessert, it's also cheap! The layer of chopped nuts, although delicious, is not essential.

If you think the almonds are too pale, you can toast them a little under the broiler, which will also intensify the flavor. To soften the nougat so you can work with it, pop it in the oven for a few minutes. Roll it out very thinly on an oiled baking sheet using a wooden rolling pin. You can form the warm nougat into lots of different shapes.

Depending on the time of year you can use white peaches instead of the kiwi fruit. Whichever you choose, the fruit's gentle acidity will refresh the taste buds.

*To make the mazarin, beat the egg yolks in a food mixer. At the same time, melt the sugar for 5–7 minutes, until a syrup forms. Beat the syrup into the eggs and leave the mixture to cool.*

*Beat the cream until stiff. Carefully fold the nougat, the crumbled wafers, and the egg mixture into the cream.*

*Line a baking sheet with plastic film and spoon the mixture into 4 round ring molds, each measuring 3 in/8 cm in diameter and 2½ in/6 cm tall. Freeze for a minimum of 5 hours, but preferably overnight.*

# with Mango Coulis

To make the chopped nut topping, melt the sugar with the lemon juice, until a caramel forms. Stir in the chopped almonds. Roll out the nut mixture, leave it to cool, then crumble the equivalent of 4 tbsp. Put everything to one side for the garnish.

To make the chocolate frosting, melt the chocolate in a double boiler, or in a bowl over a saucepan of simmering water. Spread a thin layer of chocolate over the mazarins, ensuring that it doesn't run down the sides.

Sprinkle the chopped nut topping over the mazarins. For the mango coulis, peel the mango, purée it, then pass it through a sieve to obtain a smooth sauce. Add the Grand Marnier. Peel and slice the kiwi fruit. Arrange the sliced kiwi around the mazarins. Garnish with the mango coulis.

# Pear

Preparation time:     15 minutes
Resting time:     30 minutes
Cooking time:     20 minutes
Difficulty:     ★

**Serves 4**

| | |
|---|---|
| 2 | pears |
| 1 handful | raisins |
| ⅛ stick/15 g | butter |
| 1 tbsp | sugar |
| 2 tsp/10 ml | pear brandy (e.g. Poire William) |
| ½ cup/50 g | flaked almonds |

**For the pancake batter:**

| | |
|---|---|
| 1 generous cup/125 g | all-purpose flour |
| 1 pinch | salt |

| | |
|---|---|
| 3 tbsp/50 g | superfine sugar |
| 3 | eggs |
| 2 cups/500 ml | milk |
| | grated zest of 1 unwaxed orange |
| | grated zest of 1 unwaxed lemon |

**For the custard:**

| | |
|---|---|
| 1 cup/250 ml | milk |
| 3 | egg yolks |
| 3 heaped tbsp/ 55 g | superfine sugar |

**For the garnish:**

| | |
|---|---|
| 1 | unwaxed orange |

Francis Robin's recipe for pear pancakes (*pannequets*) is a reminder of his past. Even as a novice chef, this *Maître Cuisinier de France* shone at preparing pancakes.

*Pannequet* was originally the term used for a sweet or savory pancake filled with ground meat or poultry, fruit purée, or custard. They often appear on menus, whether as appetizers, hot hors d'oeuvres or, as we suggest, a sweet dessert, because they are perfect for guests and are very easy to prepare.

Francis Robin lets the batter rest for 30 minutes, but you could leave it for an hour. Use a non-stick pan to prevent the pancakes sticking. After you have made each pancake, wipe out the skillet with kitchen paper coated with oil.

Because pears and almonds are a marriage made in heaven, it is only natural that they both appear in Francis

Robin's recipe. The best variety of pear for this dessert is Conference, available in the fall. It is not very rounded, and has a smooth, green skin with a pale reddish tinge. The slightly acidic flavor of the pear emphasizes the sweetness of the custard. If you can't find Conference pears, use Williams instead.

Francis Robin suggests that you prepare this dessert during the Christmas and New Year holidays using filberts, chopped almonds, pine nuts, or dates. Omitting the alcohol will not impair this recipe. Our chef's final tip for success is to cook the pancakes at the very last minute, because they taste best hot!

*To make the custard, bring the milk to the boil. In the meantime, beat together the egg yolks and sugar until foaming. Pour the hot milk onto the egg mixture, stirring all the time. Pour the custard into a saucepan, and cook on gentle heat, stirring all the time, until it thickens.*

*To make the pancake batter, put the flour in a bowl with a pinch of salt. Add the sugar and 3 eggs and beat in the milk. Stir in the grated orange and lemon zest. Leave the batter to rest for 30 minutes before cooking the pancakes.*

*Peel and core the pears. Dice the flesh finely. In the meantime soak the raisins in hot water to plump them up.*

# Pancakes

Melt 2 tsp butter in a skillet. Sweat the diced pear with the sugar and pear brandy, if desired.

As soon as the alcohol has evaporated, add the drained raisins and flaked almonds, and stir them into the pear mixture. Cook the pancakes in the remaining butter in another skillet.

Fill the pancakes with the pear mixture. Shape the pancakes into a little parcel and tie the top with a strand of orange zest. Spoon the custard onto the plate and sit the warm pancakes on top of the custard.

# Red Berry Compôte with

| Preparation time: | 30 minutes |
| Time for the | |
|     ice cream to infuse: | 4 hours |
| Cooking time: | 20 minutes |
| Difficulty: | ★ |

**Serves 4**

**For the red berry compôte:**

| ½ cup/100 g | pine nuts |
| 2 cups/200 g | strawberries |
| 1 generous cup/ | |
| 125 g | raspberries |
| scant ½ cup/50 g | blackberries |
| scant ¼ cup/20 g | redcurrants |
| 4 tsp/20 g | honey |

| generous ⅛ stick/20 g | butter |
| ⅓ cup + 1½ tbsp/ | |
| 100 ml | maraschino |

**For the syrup:**

| 1 generous cup/ | |
| 250 g | superfine sugar |
| 1 | vanilla bean |

**For the lemon verbena ice cream:**

| 3 | egg yolks |
| 3 heaped tbsp/ | |
| 50 g | superfine sugar |
| ⅔ cup/150 ml | milk |
| 1 sprig | fresh lemon verbena |
| ⅓ cup + 1½ tbsp/ | |
| 100 ml | heavy cream |

**For the garnish:**

| 4 | mint leaves |

Provençal red berry compôte with lemon verbena ice cream is an original recipe by our chef. This recipe, redolent of summer, is a true delicacy.

All small, red berry fruit are soft and bruise easily. They must be handled carefully and can only be transported in rigid, closed containers. Choose fruit that are not overripe and use them soon after purchase. Depending on the time of year, you could also use wild strawberries, strawberry tree (or arbutus) fruit, cranberries, or cherries.

Maraschino is a liqueur made from sweetened brandy produced from the pits of maraschino cherries. Maraschino is used predominantly for confectionery, quality desserts, and pastries. You could use a cherry liqueur instead.

Joël Garault got the idea of making lemon verbena ice cream one day when his mother-in-law gave him a lemon

verbena plant as a present. Our chef wanted to find a culinary use for this plant from the verbena family, primarily known for its medicinal properties. The leaves and flowers of perfumed verbena are used to make a herb tea that prevents liver and kidney problems. If you're lucky enough to have lemon verbena growing in your garden, garnish the ice cream with verbena flowers rather than mint leaves, depending on the time of year. You can also finely chop a couple of the flowers and cook them with the berries.

The dessert gets texture from the toasted pine nuts. They are rich in carbohydrates and lipids and are therefore a good source of energy. Their spicy, resinous flavor is reminiscent of almonds. You could also use dry cookies to add crunch to the dish.

*To make the lemon verbena ice cream, beat together the egg yolks and sugar until frothy. Bring the milk to the boil, and add the lemon verbena and egg mixture. Bring the custard to the boil, stirring all the time, and stir in the cream. Leave the custard to infuse for 4 hours.*

*Strain the custard and transfer it to an ice cream maker. To make the sugar syrup, bring 2 cups/500 ml water to the boil with the sugar and vanilla bean, then leave it to cool. Remove the vanilla bean and put to one side.*

*Dry roast the pine nuts in a hot skillet. As soon as they have browned, crush them with one strawberry.*

# Lemon Verbena Ice Cream

To make the red berry compôte, wash and hull the raspberries, strawberries, blackberries, and redcurrants. Melt the honey and butter in a saucepan and cook until a caramel forms.

Cut the strawberries in half, then toss them in the caramel with the other fruit.

Deglaze the fruit with the maraschino and sugar syrup, then heat the fruit on low heat for 5 minutes. To serve, place a scoop of the ice cream on a bed of crushed pine nuts, and garnish it with a sprig of mint. Spoon the red berry compôte onto the plate around the ice cream.

# Honeyed Pears

Preparation time: 35 minutes
Time for the
    ice cream to infuse: 4 hours
Cooking time: 20 minutes
Difficulty: ☆

**Serves 4**

| | |
|---|---|
| 4 | dessert pears |
| scant ½ stick/ | |
| 40 g | butter |
| 4 tsp/20 g | acacia honey |
| | juice of 3 oranges |
| 1 | vanilla bean |

**For the gingerbread ice cream:**

| | |
|---|---|
| 3 | egg yolks |
| 3 tbsp/50 g | superfine sugar |

| | |
|---|---|
| ⅔ cup/150 ml | milk |
| 3½ oz/100 g | gingerbread, cubed |
| ⅓ cup + 1½ tbsp/ | |
| 100 ml | heavy cream |

**For the ginger tuiles:**

| | |
|---|---|
| scant ½ stick/ | |
| 40 g | butter |
| 1 cup/100 g | confectioner's sugar |
| 3½ tbsp/50 g | passion fruit coulis |
| scant ¼ cup/ | |
| 25 g | all-purpose flour |
| 1 oz piece/30 g | fresh root ginger |

**For the garnish:**

| | |
|---|---|
| 4 sprigs | mint |

This recipe for honeyed pears with gingerbread ice cream is our chef's very own creation. The ingredients he uses all come from the Alpes-de-Haute-Provence department of France, a region where there are lots of fruit growers and beekeepers.

In this recipe, Joël Garault uses *Vereinsdechant* dessert pears. He particularly likes them because, when cooked, they turn slightly grainy, and have melting, sweet, very juicy flesh. Use unblemished fruit with completely smooth skins that hardly give at all when squeezed.

In ancient times honey was regarded as the food of the gods. It symbolized wealth and good luck, being a food and a sacrificial offering. This liquid gold, produced by bees from the nectar in flowers, is stored in the honeycomb cells. Honey provides far more energy than sugar. Acacia honey has an especially good flavor, but if you prefer to, you could of course use another type, such as lavender honey.

An ice cream made from gingerbread! Amazing? Yes, but there's a specific reason – this ice cream lends the pears a caramelized flavor that harmonizes perfectly with the acacia honey.

This dessert is also redolent of the classic spice, ginger. The aromatic ginger root, with its characteristic taste, is used fresh, preserved in syrup, or, more frequently, dried and ground. The delicate, shaped tuiles can be baked a day in advance and stored carefully in a dry place. They are easier to prepare if the butter is at room temperature.

Give your imagination free rein when garnishing this delicious dessert.

*Ice cream: Beat the egg yolks and sugar until frothy. Bring the milk to the boil and pour it onto the egg mixture, stirring all the time. Add the cubed gingerbread and cream. Leave to infuse for 4 hours. Strain the custard to remove the gingerbread and transfer it to an ice cream maker.*

*Peel the pears, and quarter them, removing the cores and stalks.*

*Melt half of the butter in a skillet with the acacia honey and let a caramel form. Add the pear quarters and sauté them on both sides.*

# with Ice Cream

Deglaze the pears with the orange juice. Add the split vanilla bean, and cook on low heat for 5 minutes. Remove the pears and vanilla bean, and put to one side. Beat the remaining butter into the pan juices to form a sauce.

To make the tuiles, beat together the butter and confectioner's sugar. Add the passion fruit coulis, the flour, and the grated root ginger.

Line a baking sheet with parchment and spread long tongues of batter onto the paper. Bake the tuiles at 410 °F/210 °C for 4 minutes. Arrange a few pear quarters, 1 scoop ice cream, and 1 tuile on each plate. Garnish with vanilla bean and mint. Spoon a little sauce onto the plate.

# Baked Pears

Preparation time: 20 minutes
Cooking time: 15 minutes
Difficulty: ★

**Serves 4**

| | |
|---|---|
| 4 | pears (Williams) |
| ¼ cup/30 g | toasted almonds |
| ¼ cup/30 g | toasted filberts |
| 2 | dried figs |
| 2 | prunes |
| 2 | dried apricots |
| scant ⅛ stick/ 10 g | butter |

| | |
|---|---|
| 3 tbsp/50 g | raw cane sugar |
| 2 scant tbsp/ 50 g | runny lavender honey |

**For the almond cream:**

| | |
|---|---|
| ½ stick/ 60 g | butter |
| ½ cup/60 g | confectioner's sugar |
| ½ cup/60 g | ground almonds |
| generous ⅛ cup/ 20 g | all-purpose flour |
| 1 | egg |
| 2 drops | almond extract |

**For the garnish:**

| | |
|---|---|
| few sprigs | mint |

The Roman poet Virgil regarded the pear as the queen of the orchard, and we are eternally grateful to the Romans for cultivating various varieties of pear. The French, too, undoubtedly love their pears. They are found as ingredients in numerous desserts, such as *Pear Charlotte* or *Tarte Bourdaloue*, with almond cream.

It's a good thing to know that pears continue to ripen after picking. If you don't want to eat them immediately, buy slightly unripe fruit. It's best if they're the last item on your shopping list so that they're on top of your cart and the delicate flesh doesn't get bruised. Once damaged, they quickly start to rot.

For his recipe, our chef uses the widely available Williams variety, available from September to December. The variety is juicy and has a smooth, green skin, with slightly reddish cheeks. The flesh is delicate, sweet, and smells of musk. If you can't find Williams pears, you could use slightly acidic Jonagold apples.

You could cook the pears in the microwave for 3–4 minutes before baking them. Pierce them with a knife to test how soft they are. Then bake them in the oven for 8–10 minutes and caramelize them under the broiler. Use the almond extract sparingly, because too much will spoil this delicious dessert.

The combination of different types of dried fruit and nuts is called *mendiants*, "beggars," in France. We use apricots and prunes instead of the customary raisins.

Peel the pears without removing the stalks. Scoop out the core using an apple corer or melon baller. Wrap the pears in plastic film so they don't discolor.

To make the almond cream, beat together the softened butter, confectioner's sugar, ground almonds, flour, and egg. Add a couple of drops of almond extract and mix well.

Preheat the oven to 320 °F/160 °C. Chop the almonds, filberts, dried figs, prunes, and dried apricots.

# with Dried Fruit

Put all the dried fruit in a bowl, add the almond cream, and mix well until completely combined.

Using a small spoon, fill the pears with the fruit mixture. Melt the butter.

Brush the pears with the melted butter and sprinkle them with raw cane sugar. Bake the pears for 15 minutes, then brown them under the broiler. Drizzle the runny honey over a plate. Place a pear in the middle of the plate, on the honey, and garnish the pear with a sprig of mint.

# Baked Apples with

Preparation time: 20 minutes
Raisin soaking
   time: 30 minutes
Cooking time: 30 minutes
Difficulty: ★

**Serves 4**

| | |
|---|---|
| 4 | Golden Delicious apples |
| scant ¼ cup/ 50 g | raisins |
| 3½ tbsp/50 ml | Calvados (or apple brandy) |
| ½ stick/55 g | butter |

| | |
|---|---|
| generous ⅔ cup/ 150 g | superfine sugar |
| ¼ cup/50 g | pine nuts |
| generous ¾ cup/ 200 ml | milk |
| 1 | vanilla bean |
| 3½ tbsp/50 ml | light cream |
| 1 generous cup/ 50 g | yellow cornmeal |
| 4 scoops | vanilla ice cream |

**For the sweetened whipped cream:**

| | |
|---|---|
| generous ¾ cup/ 200 ml | heavy cream |
| ⅛ cup/15 g | confectioner's sugar |

Baked apples with vanilla polenta is an elegant dessert for gourmets. Our chef's creation combines ingredients from the Mediterranean coast and the Normandy hills.

There's no doubt that apples are found almost everywhere throughout the world, and they are sold all year round. Our chef has chosen the variety Golden Delicious for this dessert. It is golden yellow, and has a smooth skin, and juicy, crisp, yellow flesh. Lovers of this variety particularly like the delicate, sweet flavor with a hint of acidity.

Many apple recipes are prepared with Calvados. As far as Daniel Ettlinger is concerned, apple brandy from Normandy is an integral part of his recipe. The raisins are soaked in the Calvados for an exceptional flavor.

In fact it's the raisins that form the link between the Mediterranean coast and the north of France. Our chef

prefers using them to golden raisins, because small, dark, seedless raisins have a characteristic taste.

The cornmeal harks back to Provençal roots. Although this cornmeal, mainly used in hearty dishes, originally came from northern Italy, it is very common in dishes from the Nice area. You could also make this dessert using wheatmeal. The spicy, resinous flavor of pine nuts is similar to that of almonds, which can be used instead.

You need sweetened whipped cream, also known as Chantilly cream, for this recipe. Using a hand blender or balloon whisk, beat the cream until very stiff, then fold in the confectioner's sugar just before serving.

Peel the apples. Cut them in half and remove the cores. Soak the raisins in the Calvados for 30 minutes.

Grease a deep baking dish with butter and sprinkle over a little sugar. Place the apples in the dish, core side up.

Sprinkle 3 heaped tbsp/50 g sugar over the apples and bake them in the oven for 30 minutes at 470 °F/250 °C. Toast the pine nuts in a saucepan over low heat with 2 tbsp sugar. Stir until the pine nuts have browned.

# Vanilla Polenta

To make the cornmeal, put the milk, vanilla bean, cream, and remaining sugar in a saucepan and bring to the boil. Beat in the cornmeal, and cook for 20 minutes on low heat, stirring continuously.

Drain the raisins. Deglaze the baked apples with the Calvados and put them to one side. Beat the cream.

Chop the raisins and add to the cornmeal. Use a ring mold to make a circle of cornmeal on a plate. Place half an apple on top, core side down. Add a spoon of sweetened whipped cream. Garnish with toasted pine nuts and raisins. Serve with ice cream and the Calvados sauce.

# Fruit Ratatouille

| | |
|---|---|
| *Preparation time:* | *1 hour 30 minutes* |
| *Cooking time:* | *15 minutes* |
| *Difficulty:* | ★★ |

**Serves 4**

| | |
|---|---|
| 4 | fresh figs |

**For the ginger sorbet:**

| | |
|---|---|
| 3½ oz/100 g piece | root ginger |
| scant ½ cup/100 g | superfine sugar |
| 1 tbsp | ginger syrup |
| 1 | lemon |
| 1 tsp/5 g | glucose |

**For the fruit ratatouille:**

| | |
|---|---|
| a few | strawberries, raspberries |
| 1 each | apple, pear, orange, grapefruit, mango, banana |
| some | preserved tomatoes |
| 1 | pomegranate |
| 1 | lemon |
| 1 handful each | white/black grapes |
| 1 each | pineapple, passion fruit |

**For the fruit sauce:**

| | |
|---|---|
| 1 each | pink grapefruit, orange, pear, apple |
| a few | strawberries, raspberries |
| 1 each | passion fruit, lemon |
| scant ⅓ cup/ 70 g | superfine sugar |
| a few sprigs | fresh dill |
| 1 tbsp/15 g | pectin |

**For the garnish:**

| | |
|---|---|
| a few sprigs | fresh mint |
| some | raspberries |
| a few sprigs | fresh dill |

Ratatouille is actually a vegetable stew, a typical Provençal dish from the Nice area. Our chef has reinvented the recipe and has turned it into a dessert created with a wealth of delicious fruits.

Be prepared for a laborious task when preparing this dessert, because finely chopping the fruit takes a long time. Chop the fruit carefully, so that they will all be of the same consistency. When you make the sauce, the fruit is all passed through a sieve, so you don't need to peel it.

Figs are important in this dessert, so bear in mind that they will only keep for 24 hours. Ripe figs have fine cracks on the skin's surface and give a little when squeezed. They should not give too much, though, otherwise they are overripe. A firm stalk is a good indication of their freshness. Use a small melon baller to hollow out the figs. Reserve the fig flesh because it will be chopped and added to the sauce at a later stage.

Dill is an umbelliferous plant that originated in the Far East. It is also known as "false aniseed" or "bastard fennel" and was a symbol of vitality in Ancient Rome.

Ginger is used in the sorbet. Ginger comes from India, Malaysia, and other countries where the weather is very hot. As long ago as the Middle Ages, plants from the ginger family, including Siamese ginger, or galangal, and cardamom, were very popular. The aromatic roots are candied, or dried, and ground to make a powder. If the ginger flavor in the sorbet is too strong, or the sorbet is too sweet, add a few drops of lemon juice. Garnish the plates with a few strawberries.

*Wash all the fruit and very finely dice enough of each to make a heaped tablespoonful. Remove the pips from the grapes. Keep a little of the diced fruit to garnish the figs. Use the remaining fruit for the sauce.*

*Peel the root ginger, cut it into strips, and blanch it. Boil 4 cups/1 l water with the sugar, then add the chopped ginger. Boil gently until a syrup forms. Make a sorbet from the candied ginger, 2 cups/500 ml water, and the other ingredients. Transfer to an ice cream maker and freeze it.*

*Wash the fruit for the sauce and chop finely. Scoop the flesh out of the figs and add the fig flesh to the fruit for the sauce. Purée the fruit and sieve it.*

# with Ginger

Add sugar and 4 tsp/20 g chopped dill to the reserved, diced fruit.

Purée the remaining diced fruit not used in the ratatouille and sieved fruit purée using a hand blender set to maximum. Don't forget to add the pectin.

Carefully fill the figs with the fruit ratatouille and place each one on a slice of ginger sorbet. Pour the fruit sauce around the ice cream and garnish with sprigs of dill.

# Mama Conchita's

| | |
|---|---|
| Preparation time: | 20 minutes |
| Time for the wine | |
| sorbet to infuse: | 4 hours |
| Soaking time: | 2 hours |
| Cooking time: | 1 hour |
| Difficulty: | ★★ |

**Serves 4**

| | |
|---|---|
| ½ cup/100 g | short grain/pudding rice |
| 2 cups/500 ml | milk |
| 1 | vanilla bean |
| | peel of 1 unwaxed |
| | orange, in one piece |
| 8 strands | saffron |
| 4 tbsp/60 g | superfine sugar |

| | |
|---|---|
| ⅓ cup + 1½ tbsp/ | |
| 100 ml | light cream |
| 2 | egg yolks |

| | |
|---|---|
| 6 | dried figs |
| 3½ tbsp/50 ml | Banyuls |
| **For the spiced wine sorbet:** | |
| 1 | orange |
| 5 | black peppercorns |
| ½ | cinnamon stick |
| 1 | clove |
| 5 | juniper berries |
| 1 pinch | ground nutmeg |
| scant ½ cup/ | |
| 100 g | superfine sugar |
| 1¼ cups/300 ml | red wine |
| **For the garnish:** | |
| 4 sprigs | fresh mint |
| 24 | raspberries |

Jean-Claude Vila has fond memories of the rice pudding his mother used to make for him. Mama Conchita was a superb cook and enriched the ingredients for this dessert with saffron, which is primarily used in *paella*. This family recipe brings to mind memories of favorite childhood dishes. When he went to school, he was allowed to eat toasted bread over which Conchita had drizzled a little of the spiced wine.

After wheat, rice is the most widely cultivated cereal in the world. It grows in marshy or very damp ground and has been cultivated in China for over 5,000 years.

When combined with saffron, the rice pudding has a very delicate flavor, provided exactly the right amount of saffron is added. Saffron is famed for its spicy scent and bitter taste, and there is nothing quite like it. The stamens of this bulbous member of the crocus family supply this renowned spice, in the form of brown threads, or yellowish-red powder. The other spices, many of them from the East, were for centuries reserved for the kitchens of the nobility. Happily that has all changed. Spiced wine is a Catalan specialty and here forms the basis of the sorbet. It should definitely be made the day before the sorbet, and should include at least one of the named spices.

Banyuls, used here to flavor the figs, is an A.O.C. (*Appellation d'Origine Controlée*) wine, whose production is subject to strict regulations. This sweet, fortified wine (*vin doux naturel*) bears the name of the town in Roussillon where it is made, and is a popular French aperitif. If you cannot get hold of Banyuls, you could use another sweet fortified wine instead.

*To make the wine sorbet, quarter the orange, and then cut each quarter in half again. Put the orange in a pan with all the spices, the sugar, and the wine. Cover the pan and warm on low heat; do not boil. Leave to infuse for 4 hours. Strain and pour the wine into the ice cream maker.*

*Precook the rice, adding enough water to just cover it. Boil for 5 minutes, then drain the rice and rinse it.*

*Simmer the rice for 20 minutes with the milk, the split vanilla bean, and the orange peel.*

# Rice Pudding

Add the saffron, cover the pan, and simmer for another 5 minutes. Remove the orange peel, and vanilla bean, and reserve them for the garnish.

Add the sugar, some of the cream, and egg yolks to the rice. Stir well, and take the pan off the heat.

Place the figs in boiling water. Take the pan off the heat and soak the figs for 2 hours. Cut off the stalks, then purée the figs. Add the Banyuls wine and remaining cream. Arrange some of the rice pudding, a scoop of sorbet, and fig purée on a plate. Garnish with mint and raspberries.

# Fennel Sorbet with

Preparation time: 1 hour 30 minutes
Resting time for
    the tuile batter: 1 hour
Time for syrup
    to infuse: 1 hour
Cooking time: 25 minutes
Difficulty: ★

**Serves 4**

**For the syrup:**
| | |
|---|---|
| 5 tsp/25 g | glucose |
| 1 tsp | honey |
| 1 cup + 1 tbsp/ 240 g | superfine sugar |
| ¾ cup/125 g | fennel seeds |

**For the tuiles:**
| | |
|---|---|
| scant ¼ stick/25 g | butter |
| scant 2 tbsp/25 g | superfine sugar |

| | |
|---|---|
| 1 tbsp/25 g | raw cane sugar |
| scant ¼ cup/ 25 g | all-purpose flour |
| ⅓ cup + 1½ tbsp/ 100 ml | orange juice |
| 2 tsp/10 g | fennel seeds |

**For the saffron custard:**
| | |
|---|---|
| 1 cup/250 ml | milk |
| 3 | egg yolks |
| 3 heaped tbsp/ 50 g | superfine sugar |
| 1 pinch | saffron |

**For the garnish:**
| | |
|---|---|
| | saffron threads |
| | fresh fennel leaves |

Fennel sorbet with saffron custard is chef Christian Étienne's own creation. One day he decided to create a dessert using fennel, and then looked around for a sauce that would provide a suitable accompaniment. His imagination immediately led this connoisseur of *haute cuisine* to a custard with saffron, and a dessert with a truly amazing taste was born.

Fennel is usually used with fish in France. This bulbous vegetable with its tightly packed leaves is generally eaten as a vegetable, and as such should be firm, with an unblemished white color.

Crush the fennel seeds with a rolling pin. You could also used chopped filberts or almonds for the *tuiles*. To save time, our chef prepares the syrup a day in advance. If you would like to emphasize the delicate aniseed flavor of fennel further, you could add a dash of lemon juice before transferring the syrup to the ice cream maker. And if you don't like the rather bitter flavor of saffron, our chef suggests you try a vanilla custard.

*Tuiles* are easier to make if the butter is at room temperature. If you don't have any baking parchment or silicon-coated baking paper, you could always bake them direct on a well-greased and floured baking sheet.

The *tuiles* get their characteristic shape from being rolled around a rolling pin while still warm, but take care, because they are very brittle and break easily!

Our chef arranges the *tuiles* on scoops of sorbet sitting on a pool of saffron custard.

*Make the syrup using 1 cup/250 ml water, the glucose, and honey. Add the sugar and bring to the boil.*

*Add the fennel seeds and 1 cup/250 ml water. Leave the syrup to infuse for 1 hour or more.*

*Saffron custard: Boil the milk. Beat the egg yolks and sugar until frothy, then stir in the hot milk. Pour the custard back into the saucepan and gently cook until it thickens. As soon as it comes to the boil, take the pan off the burner. Add the saffron into the custard, beating well.*

# Saffron Custard

Strain the syrup through a sieve and adjust to taste. Pour the syrup into an ice cream maker to make a sorbet. Scoop out balls of sorbet, and store these in the freezer.

In a bowl beat together the softened butter and sugar. Add the raw cane sugar, and then the flour and orange juice, stirring all the time. Beat the batter until smooth, then leave it to rest for 1 hour.

Spread circles of batter on the baking parchment and sprinkle over crushed fennel seeds. Bake for 5 minutes at 350 °F/180 °C. Curve the tuiles with a rolling pin. Pour some custard onto a plate, and place three scoops of sorbet on top. Garnish with tuiles, saffron, and fennel.

| Preparation time: | 30 minutes |
|---|---|
| Resting time: | 2 hours |
| Cooking time: | 15 minutes |
| Difficulty: | ★ |

**Serves 4**

| 10 | fresh figs |
|---|---|
| generous ⅛ cup/ 40 g | raw cane sugar |

**For the plain pastry:**

| 2 cups/250 g | all-purpose flour |
|---|---|
| 1 generous cup/ 125 g | confectioner's sugar |
| 1 tsp/5 g | baking powder |

| scant 1⅛ sticks/ 125 g | butter |
|---|---|
| 1 | egg |

| 1 pinch | salt |
|---|---|
| | grated zest of 1 orange |
| | grated zest of 1 lemon |

**For the almond cream:**

| scant 1⅛ sticks/ 120 g | butter |
|---|---|
| 1 generous cup/ 120 g | confectioner's sugar |
| 1 generous cup/ 120 g | ground almonds |
| ⅓ cup/40 g | all-purpose flour |
| 2 | eggs |
| 2 drops | almond extract |

Georges Rousset's fresh fig tart is a jewel of the pastry chef's art, where fruit is king. This dessert is special because of its simplicity, and in fact is based on a traditional Languedoc recipe. Surrounded by a square of plain pastry, the majestic fig reclines on a bed of almond cream.

The popularity of the fig, this delicate Mediterranean fruit, has not waned over the years. From the dawn of civilization it was honored by the Mediterranean cultures as a symbol of fertility. The best time for figs is mid-June to mid-July, and then again from August to the start of November. You cannot tell whether a fig is ripe from its color, but by feeling it carefully. Figs do not keep well and can be stored in the refrigerator for only a day or so.

The zest of citrus fruit is used a lot in cooking and baking. It is easy to remove the outer layer of skin and dry it in the open air. You should only buy organic, unwaxed oranges

and lemons. Take great care when adding the almond extract, because it can spoil the taste of the cream. Extract of bitter almond has a very powerful flavor and is made from the pits of the bitter almond.

The almond tree likes a dry, hot climate and therefore flourishes through the Mediterranean area, where it is regarded as a symbol of wealth, knowledge, and fruitfulness. Ground almonds are popular for use in baking. Whether accompanied by honey, as in the North African countries, or by pears, as in France's *Tarte Bourdaloue* or *Galette des Rois*, almonds will always appeal to gourmets.

*Sift the flour onto a work surface. Sprinkle the confectioner's sugar and baking powder on top. Cut the butter into small pieces and rub into the dry ingredients. Add the egg, salt, grated orange and lemon zest. Bring the dough together into a ball and leave to rest for 2 hours.*

*To make the almond cream, beat the softened butter, sugar, ground almonds, flour, and eggs using an electric mixer. Add 2 drops of almond extract and mix together well.*

*Dust a pastry board or work surface with flour and roll out the pastry. Using a pastry wheel, cut the pastry into squares with sides 4–4½ in/10–12 cm long. Prick the pastry squares all over with a fork. Preheat the oven to 320 °F/160 °C.*

# Fig Tart

Using your fingers, pinch around the edges of the pastry to form a rim that is ¼–½ in/1 cm high all around.

Spread a layer of almond cream over the squares, and bake them in the oven for 5 minutes. Let the pastry cool a little. Slice the figs lengthwise.

Arrange overlapping layers of fig slices on the pastry squares, then bake them for another 5 minutes. Sprinkle 1 tbsp raw cane sugar over each fig tart and bake them in the oven for a further 3–5 minutes.

# Pine Nut Tart with

Preparation time: 25 minutes
Resting time: 1 hour
Cooking time: 20 minutes
Difficulty: ★

**Serves 4**

| | |
|---|---|
| 1 scant stick/100 g | butter |
| scant ½ cup/100 g | sugar |
| 2 level tbsp/60 g | lavender honey |
| 1¾ cups/400 g | pine nuts |
| 2 cups/500 ml | light cream |

**For the plain pastry:**

| | |
|---|---|
| generous ½ cup/125 g | superfine sugar |
| scant 1⅛ sticks/125 g | butter |
| 1 pinch | salt |
| 2 cups/250 g | all-purpose flour |
| 1 | egg |

In Provence, a day when this pine nut tart with lavender honey is on the menu is no ordinary day ... It's a special day for children who love to eat this delicious dessert when they come home from school. This typical, southern French dessert is best served after a light main course.

Pine nuts are rich in carbohydrates and lipids and are therefore a good source of energy. Their spicy, resinous flavor is reminiscent of almonds, which can be used instead. These little, elongated nuts come from the cones of the stone pine, a tree from the Abietacea family, which grows in the Mediterranean area. They are surrounded by a hard casing and lie between the pine cone's scales.

Here's a tip from Christian Étienne to ensure perfect plain pastry every time: Bake the pastry case for ten minutes, covering it with baking parchment weighted with dried peas, lentils, or navy beans, so that the pastry doesn't rise.

Then add the caramelized pine nut filling, and bake the tart for another 15 minutes.

In ancient times, honey was regarded as the food of the gods. It symbolized wealth and good fortune, being a food and a sacrificial offering. This pine nut tart is a wonderful way to make the most of its flavor. Honey is produced by bees from the nectar in flowers, and is stored in the honeycomb cells. Honey provides far more energy than sugar. Lavender honey comes from Provence, where the whole countryside is drenched in the scent of these lilac-colored flowers. You could use another type of honey if you prefer.

Usually, in France, just a cup of tea or a hot chocolate is served with this dessert.

Pastry: Mix the sugar and butter by hand. Sift the flour and salt onto a work surface. Put the egg and also the butter mixture in the middle. Knead the ingredients together with the fingertips to form dough. Shape it into a ball, dredge it in flour, and leave to rest for 1 hour.

Grease the tart pan. Roll out the pastry and line a springform pan with it. Place the pan on a baking sheet.

Melt the butter in a copper saucepan. Add the sugar and honey, and cook until a pale caramel forms.

# Lavender Honey

Add the pine nuts. Stir them well until they are caramelized.

Add the cream to the pan and stir very well.

Pour the pine nut mixture into the pastry case and bake it for 15 minutes at 350 °F/180 °C. Remove the tart from the springform pan while it is still warm.

# Melon Tartlet

Preparation time: 45 minutes
Resting time: 1 hour
Cooking time: 20 minutes
Difficulty: ★★

**Serves 4**

| | |
|---|---|
| 2 | honeydew melons |
| 3 tbsp scant | grenadine syrup |
| ⅛ stick/10 g | butter |
| ⅓ cup + 1½ tbsp/ 100 ml | Muscatel wine |

**For the plain pastry:**

| | |
|---|---|
| scant ½ cup/50 g | ground almonds |
| 2 generous cups/250 ml | all-purpose flour |
| 3⅓ cups/750 g | superfine sugar |
| 1¾ sticks/190 g | diced butter |
| | zest of 1 unwaxed lemon |
| 3 | eggs |
| 3 tsp | dark rum |
| 1 pinch | salt |

**For the confectioner's custard with Muscatel:**

| | |
|---|---|
| 2 cups/500 ml | full fat milk |
| 1 | vanilla bean |
| 6 | eggs |
| ½ cup + 1 tbsp/ 125 g | superfine sugar |
| 4 tsp/20 g | cornstarch |
| generous ⅜ cup/ 50 g | all-purpose flour |
| 2 envelopes | gelatin |
| 3½ tbsp/50 ml | Muscatel wine |
| ½ cup/120 ml | cream |

**For the sugar syrup:**

| | |
|---|---|
| ⅔ cup/150 g | superfine sugar |

**For the garnish:**

| | |
|---|---|
| ⅛ cup/15 g | confectioner's sugar |
| few sprigs | fresh mint |

This refreshing dessert is the perfect way to round off a summer meal, as melon, with which the delicate pastry is filled, is at its best in summer. The dessert's name is a homage to Bel Air, one of the suburbs of the town of Salon-de-Provence.

To recognize a good melon you must weigh it in your hand. It must feel heavy, but give a little if you press with your thumb at the stalk end. The stalk should be easy to remove and the melon should be perfumed. If the melon smell is very strong, then the fruit is probably overripe. Skin colors vary from light green, through striped dark green and bright yellow, to reddish-green, with a smooth or rough skin.

Melons will keep for 5–6 days in a cool, well-ventilated place. It's best not to store them in the refrigerator, because their perfume can transfer to other foods. If stored at room temperature, melons continue to ripen a little.

For this recipe we recommend a smooth-skinned honeydew melon, with its sweet, juicy, firm flesh. Use a melon baller to get even-sized balls. Instead of making a stock syrup yourself, you can always use sugar cane or sugar beet syrup to cook the melon balls.

Don't knead the pastry for too long, otherwise it will become tough. To rest it, shape it into a long roll, about the size of a rolling pin. Then it's easy to roll out slices of pastry ready for cutting. You can always use ready-made rich plain pastry, from the supermarket. You will need a 14 ounce/400 gram package.

---

*To make the plain pastry, combine the ground almonds, flour, sugar, grated zest of ½ lemon, and a pinch of salt. Add the diced, softened butter, 2 egg yolks, 1 egg, and the rum.*

*Cut the roll of pastry into 1 in/3 cm-thick slices. Roll out each slice of pastry and cut out circles 3 in/8 cm in diameter. Bake the pastry circles in the oven for 10 minutes at 400 °F/200 °C. Soften the gelatin in water.*

*Confectioner's custard: Boil the milk with the vanilla bean. Beat together 4 egg yolks, 2 eggs, the sugar, and the cornstarch. Add the flour in a steady trickle, beating all the time. Stir in half the milk. Pour the custard into the milk in the pan. Simmer for 5 minutes, stirring all the time.*

# "Bel Air"

Take the pan off the heat. Drain the gelatin and beat it into the custard. Add the Muscatel wine, mix well, then leave the custard to cool. Beat the cream until stiff, fold it carefully into the custard, then put it aside.

In a saucepan combine 1 cup/250 ml water and 3 heaped tbsp/150 g sugar. Boil the solution for 2–3 minutes until a colorless syrup forms. Put aside. Scoop out 32 melon balls. Make a sauce from the melon flesh by puréeing it with the grenadine syrup and 2 tbsp sugar syrup.

Sweat the melon balls in the butter. Add 7 tbsp sugar syrup and the Muscatel wine. Drain. Spread 2 pastry rounds with confectioner's custard, then sandwich the melon balls between them. Dust with sifted confectioner's sugar. Garnish with mint sprigs and the melon sauce.

**Laurent Broussier**

**Alain Carro**

**Christian Étienne**

**Daniel Ettlinger**

**Joël Garrault**

**Jean-Michel Minguella**

# Chefs

**Jean Plouzennec**

**Francis Robin**

**Georges Rousset**

**Jean-Claude Vila**

**Angel Yagues**

**Abbreviations:**

1 oz = 1 ounce = 28 grams
1 lb = 1 pound = 16 ounces
1 cup = 8 ounces* (see below)
1 cup = 8 fluid ounces = 250 milliliters (liquids)
2 cups = 1 pint (liquids)
1 tbsp = 1 level tablespoon = 15-20 g* (see below) = 15 milliliters (liquids)
1 tsp = 1 level teaspoon = 3-5 g* (see below) = 5 ml (liquids)
1 kg = 1 kilogram = 1000 grams
1 g = 1 gram = $\frac{1}{1000}$ kilogram
1 l = 1 liter = 1000 milliliters = approx. 34 fluid ounces
1 ml = 1 milliliter = $\frac{1}{1000}$ liter

*The weight of dry ingredients varies significantly depending on the density factor, e.g. 1 cup flour weighs less than 1 cup butter. Quantities in ingredients have been rounded up or down for convenience, where appropriate. Metric conversions may therefore not correspond exactly. It is important to use either American or metric measurements within a recipe.

© Original edition copyright: Fabien BELLAHSEN and Daniel ROUCHE

Concept and production: Fabien Bellahsen, Daniel Rouche
Photography and technical direction: Didier Bizos
Photographic assistant: Gersende Petit-Jouvet
Editors: Élodie Bonnet, Nathalie Talhouas
Editorial assistant: Fabienne Ripon
Consultant: Jean Bordier

Original title: *Délices du Sud de la France*
ISBN of the original edition: 2-84308-355-9
ISBN-10 of the German edition: 3-8331-1088-0
ISBN-13 of the German edition: 978-3-8331-1088-7

© 2006 for the English edition:
Tandem Verlag GmbH
KÖNEMANN is a trademark and an imprint of Tandem Verlag GmbH

Translation from German:
Karen Green for First Edition Translations Ltd, Cambridge, UK
Editing: Jenny Knight for First Edition Translations Ltd
Typesetting and project management: First Edition Translations Ltd

Project coordinator: Isabel Weiler

Printed in China

ISBN-10: 3-8331-2029-0
ISBN-13: 978-3-8331-2029-9

10 9 8 7 6 5 4 3 2 1
X IX VIII VII VI V IV III II I